Sid,

God's family
    is perfect!

D Jues

"I'm 30, I'm Single, and I Don't Care!"

JULIETTE BUSH

Unless otherwise stated, all Scripture quotations are taken from *the Holy Bible*, New Living Translation, copyright © 1996, 2004, 2015 by Tyndale House Foundation. Used by permission of Tyndale House Publishers, Inc., Carol Stream, Illinois 60188. All rights reserved.

Scripture quotations marked (NIV) are taken from The Holy Bible, New International Version® NIV®
Copyright © 1973, 1978, 1984, 2011 by Biblica, Inc.
Used by permission. All rights reserved worldwide.

Scripture quotations marked (ESV) are from The Holy Bible, English Standard Version®
(ESV®),
Copyright © 2001 by Crossway Bibles, a publishing ministry of Good News publishers.
Used by permission. All rights reserved.

Scripture quotations marked (NASAB) are taken from the NEW AMERICAN STANDARD BIBLE®, Copyright ©
1960, 1962, 1963, 1968, 1971, 1972, 1973, 1975, 1977, 1995 by The Lockman Foundation.
Used by permission. www.lockman.org

Scriptures marked KJV are taken from the KING JAMES VERSION (KJV): KING JAMES VERSION, public domain.

Righteousness. (2017). *Merriam-Webster*. Retrieved from http://www.merriam-webster.com/dictionary/Righteousness

Harmartia. (2017). *Merriam-Webster*. Retrieved from https://www.merriam-webster.com/dictionary/hamartia

Oxytocin (April, 2016). *Psychology Today*. Retrieved from https://www.psychologytoday.com/basics/oxytocin

Contentment. (2015). *Holman Illustrated Bible Dictionary, Revised and Expanded* (page 335). Nashville, TN: B&H Publishing
Group.

Editor-in-Chief: Emily Juhnke
Editor: Grace & Co. Editorial Services (Dominique Bozeman)
Cover Graphic Design: Norbert Elnar at masterpiecemovement.com
Formatting: Karolyne Roberts at TheWritersRetreat.org

*A special thanks and credit to contributing writers: Sooky Park, Serina Marie Raymond, Riley N., Arlen Gomes,
Helouise Plezens and April D. Wesley.

ISBN: 978-0-9970264-6-7
www.juliettebush.com
ALL RIGHTS RESERVED
Printed in the U.S.A

Table of Contents

Dedication

This book is for all my single ladies out there who are living their lives to the fullest.

Introduction

Yes, you read that cover right! You don't need to do a double take. Writing about this topic is dear to my heart because this is my reality: yes, I'm 30; yes, I'm single; and no, I'm not ashamed of it.

In this day and age, society often pressures women into marriage or into fantasizing about our futures. We're told we should be busy planning for and figuring out how to meet certain milestones instead of letting God provide.

Our lives are often about following a pattern: first, we graduate from high school, then college, and then perhaps we take on a summer internship before going on to start our careers. However, more often than not, our society doesn't recognize women as successful until we have romantic success. And when we do find that special someone, the questions from those around us might seem to be more about our future timelines than our actual relationships. Instead of, "How did you two meet?" or "What do you love most about the person?" it's, "When are you getting engaged?" or "When will you set a date?" Then those questions are often followed by, "When will you start a family?"

Marriage is made to seem like an accomplishment on a checklist, not a union with purpose meant to bring glory to God.

Ever since we were little, many of us have had a subconscious dream to find and get married to our prince charming. From fairytales read to us at bedtime to Disney movies we couldn't get enough of, we grew up watching and hearing about it. You know the story well by now: Cinderella has a lonely life while trying to overcome some obstacle, prince charming comes to rescue her, and they live happily ever after. We have been trained to think of marriage as an escape from life or a solution to all of our problems. Get married and everything will be all right, it seems. Weddings have been ingrained into our minds as the climax of our existence, the most important day of our lives, the greatest thing we will ever do.

On many of our vision boards, there is a wedding dress. We're taught to have a five-year, ten-year, or twenty-year plan for our lives that includes things we want to accomplish in a certain timeframe. If we don't have everything we want on our boards in the specific time we've allotted for it, we often feel like a failure. Pressure kicks in and we feel "behind" in life. We don't take time to think about what influenced our lists in the first place: comparison, societal norms, what we deemed as success, and what we would want others to envy. Because there is so much judgment from society and pressure to "get a man" at any cost, even if it's not in God's plans or timing, it's easy to become discouraged or frustrated.

I'm frequently asked why I don't have a boyfriend, why I don't have the urgency to go out to events where I might meet someone, or why I don't want to put on an over-the-top outfit to try and bait a man. If I do happen to meet and start talking to someone, the questions that follow are usually about how much money they make or what their line of work is, as if the guy is supposed to be my financial plan.

When I began to pursue traveling and living abroad, many people were concerned and thought that I should stay in one place and "settle down" so it would be easier to find Mr. Right and start a family. We are often taught to revolve our lives around making it easier to meet the man of our dreams, even if this involves making changes to our careers, purpose, and dreams for the future. It's as if our wedding day is the epitome of our value and mission on this earth.

When we're not dating, people often question that as if they need a specific reason for why we are single. In doing so, even if they don't realize it, they're basically implying that there is something wrong with us and that there needs to be an explanation for why we're currently living as an individual and not as part of a couple. We're made to feel like we're not living our own life the right way until we've found another person to validate our existence.

This breeds discontentment, frustration, and many other negative emotions that keep our eyes off of God. Instead of taking on the pressures to figure out our own lives, we should really attempt to discover what our single life is supposed to look like as children of God. How is God trying to develop you in this season? Are you available to His molding, or are you more concerned about your future husband than you are about pleasing God? We must recognize that our season of being single is absolutely vital to our season of marriage.

INTRODUCTION

The Lord has laid this book on my heart in order to share what life should look like in this season. This book isn't an A-Z in how to get a man — this book is about purpose, what to focus on in your single season, and how to be content through it all.

In this book, I will keep it real with you. We'll have a lot of candid, woman-to-woman conversation. I am writing to you as a sister. I don't want to help you cope with being single; I want you to be a successful single. My heart for this book isn't about being content just until our husband comes, but it is to lead you toward full contentment in Jesus. This means remaining content in who you are in Him even after your husband arrives or if he never shows up at all.

The Word says to go into the world and make disciples. Before we are called to anything else, we are called to be disciples of Jesus Christ. Our job as disciples is to follow Him no matter the costs. Would you still serve God even if He doesn't bring you everything you think you need or want? If He doesn't bring you a husband, would you still follow Him?

As a Christian single, I want to share with you what your life should look like now, as it will empower you for your tomorrow. Yes, God may have given you the desire to be married, but this is not supposed to be a torturous period of expectation and anticipation. Having the desire to be married is only a bad thing when it becomes an idol—something that you hold higher than God.

Before diving in, I would love to pray with you. As the Bible states in Matthew 18:20, *"For where two or three gather together as my followers, I am there among them."* The preceding verse states, *"I also tell you this: If two of you agree here on earth concerning anything you ask, my Father in heaven will do it for you"* (18:19).

When it says the Lord is here with us, although we cannot see him physically, it is the Holy Spirit that is here covering us. When we pray as two or more believers and stand in agreement together, it is more powerful than a superficial agreement of a thousand people. As we pray, our heart is that God's will be done, therefore our request will be granted. I believe the Holy Spirit is here right now, wanting to teach you something, wanting to intervene to give you hope and peace in the season that is before you.

"Lord, I pray for the person who is reading this right now. I pray for the release of any distractions that may keep them from reading this book. I thank you, Lord, for their courage to get to know You more deeply. I also thank You for their purpose that You will reveal to them for this season. I pray against any strongholds from previous relationships. I pray that You break every generational curse and any wrong way of thinking. I pray that their mind is open and their heart is pure to hear and receive from You. Lead and guide them in their walk. I pray they will know that they are appointed for the season that they are in. In Jesus' name I pray, Amen.

Chapter 1

Celebrate Your Single Season

When we think about being 30 years old, it often either frightens or excites us. Depending on what level of success you think you have obtained, this feeling might control whether you will binge eat at home while watching Netflix or look for that amazing dress to put on when the clock strikes midnight.

Your "30" could be someone else's "21" or "25." It is whatever age that *you* have imagined as your "get married, have kids, and have a successful career" age.

But is this really success to you? Why are you putting so much pressure on yourself? Is it grandma and 'nem who are making you feel this way? You can tell them to adopt a baby and brush their hair if they feel the need for you to have a village so soon.

The Definition of Success

True success as a believer is obeying God and living in His will for your life. This is based on the principle of Romans 12:2 that we do not conform to the pattern of this world. We conform to God and His ways. We are no longer living for ourselves, but we are living for Christ (2 Corinthians 5:15). If you're having thoughts that things you've done or gone through in your past can prevent you from entering into a relationship with God and the life He has planned for you, I can't emphasize enough how false that is. As scripture states in

2 Corinthians 5:17, *"Anyone who belongs to Christ has become a new person. The old life is gone; a new life has begun!"*

Obeying God requires faith because we don't know what the outcome will be. We don't know the future, but we are putting our full trust and hope in Him. To have faith is the cornerstone of this walk. What is faith, you may wonder? Hebrews 11:1 NIV defines faith as, *"confidence in what we hope for and assurance about what we do not see."* Basically, faith means to trust in something that you cannot explicitly prove. The Lord says that without faith it's impossible to please Him (Hebrews 11:6).

Do you realize that our obedience to God is better than sacrifice (1 Samuel 15:22)? It doesn't matter how many hours you've spent doing community service work, how much money you've given to the poor, or if you've cleaned a nursing home. Your obedience to Him in all things is more valuable.

Deuteronomy 8:1 says, *"Be careful to obey all the commands I am giving you today. Then you will live and multiply, and you will enter and occupy the land the Lord swore to give your ancestors."* God has made a covenant with us through Moses. When we obey Him and are living in His will, He is obligated to take care of us.

1 Kings 2:3 says, *"Observe the requirements of the LORD your God, and follow all his ways. Keep the decrees, commands, regulations, and laws written in the Law of Moses so that you will be successful in all you do and wherever you*

go." The type of "success" he is speaking of is not that of worldly means, but it is success in favor, grace, and contentment. Bringing glory to God through service to Him is the main purpose of our lives.

We work unto the Lord. We shouldn't be begging for the praise of man, but urging to hear the words, "Well done, thou good and faithful servant."

The Lord states in Psalm 84:11 that, *"He will withhold no good thing from those who do what is right."* This applies to your obedience of His commands, but He is also looking at your heart (Proverbs 16:2). Your actions and service are one thing. You can be the deacon at church, serve in five ministries, and give millions to the poor, but if your heart isn't right, that doesn't matter. The Lord sees all things and knows the intentions behind your actions.

The day of judgment is real and will take place just as it is written, although many people try to "guess," speculate, or even say it won't come in their lifetime. In Mark 13:31-33, Jesus said that information is reserved for the Father only:

"Heaven and earth will disappear, but my words will never disappear. However, no one knows the day or hour when these things will happen, not even the angels in heaven or the Son himself. Only the Father knows. And since you don't know when that time will come, be on guard! Stay alert!"

You see, His word is true and will not wash away. It's real. We have to stay on guard and on alert by being on mission about our Father's business. Jesus tells His disciples to take heed, watch, and pray so that they will not be taken by surprise and be unprepared when the day comes. We should be living our lives intentionally. This means we are not just living by the moment or by what we want or desire, but that we are living with eternity on our hearts and minds. That is our home and what we are preparing for. The earth will fade away and we are just dust, but the Kingdom of God will stand (Matthew 24:35).

The Lord teaches us how we can continuously prepare for this day in Mark 13:35-37 NIV:

"Therefore keep watch because you do not know when the owner of the house will come back — whether in the evening, or at midnight, or when the rooster crows, or at dawn. If he comes suddenly, do not let him find you sleeping. What I say to you, I say to everyone: 'Watch!'"

This is because in Matthew 25:31-34, it states:

"But when the Son of Man comes in his glory, and all the angels with him, then he will sit upon his glorious throne. All the nations will be gathered in his presence, and he will separate the people as a shepherd separates the sheep from the goats. He will place the sheep at his right hand and the goats at his left.

Then the King will say to those on his right, 'Come, you who are blessed by my Father, inherit the Kingdom prepared for you from the creation of the world.'"

You see, He will separate you if you are not living the life He called you to live.

However, He tells us in John 14:2-3:

"There is more than enough room in my Father's home. If this were not so, would I have told you that I am going to prepare a place for you? When everything is ready, I will come and get you, so that you will always be with me where I am."

So do not worry, there is a room for you. He is preparing your room as we speak. As He is preparing, that is also what we are supposed to be doing here on earth through fulfilling His great commission. As He prepares, so do we. You wouldn't want Him to stop preparing for us, would you?

Don't get this mixed up by thinking this time of preparation is a punishment, a curse, or a way of God withholding certain things from us. It absolutely is not. His thoughts and ways are higher than ours (Isaiah 55:9), and we must be content and satisfied in that. We should be asking that God's will be done, not ours.

You don't have to worry about when your next season will come into fruition, whether that's a job, a family relationship, a marriage, or a career. The great thing is that everything comes in His time (Ecclesiastes 3:1). Those things should not be our focus, but rather the byproduct of living for Him.

Fear Factor: Human Fear vs. Godly Fear

I know that the fear of aging exists, but we can't hide from it. It's time to come out of the closet and rejoice in your next birthday. If you're lying to others about your age, stop. I understand that you don't want to appear "unsuccessful" or let people down, but putting the opinions of others higher than what God speaks about you is a form of idolatry. The only fear that we should have is the fear of God, but we often seem to have more fear in what others will think of us.

"And I know that whatever God does is final. Nothing can be added to it or taken from it. God's purpose is that people should fear Him." – Ecclesiastes 3:14

To fear God means to respect and stand in awe of Him because of who He is. Purpose in life starts with Who we know, not with what we know or how good we are. **It is impossible to fulfill your God-given purpose unless you revere God and give Him first place in your life.**

Proverbs 1:7 NIV states, *"The fear of the Lord is the beginning of knowledge, but fools despise wisdom and instruction."* Do you know that you are considered a fool if you don't follow the ways of the Lord? I know that there are pressures by society, but the real fool is the one that deters from *His* ways.

God wants us to walk by faith, and Satan wants us to walk by fear. Every fear, other than the fear of God, is not of God. Fear begins with a thought. Then it shows up in our actions. Proverbs 23:7 KJV tells us that, *"For as he thinketh in his heart, so is he."*

Fear that things will not come together in His timing, fear of what others will think of us, fear that we will turn out just like someone we don't like, fear that things will never get better, fear that we won't accomplish what we were meant to do on this earth, fear of our bank accounts, fear of our employers, fear that our clock is ticking and we won't have kids if we don't hurry up and get married, fear that there is no good man out there... fear, fear, fear.

All of these fears lead to us placing false expectations on ourselves. When we don't fulfill them, the disappointment leads to comparison. And what does comparison breed? Jealousy. You might have your expectation and time table, but when you see Mary Jane on Facebook with her perfect house, car, and family, it suddenly becomes, "Oh, now where is mine?!"

The Bible shows us that when we reduce ourselves to comparing our lives and accomplishments to those of others, we end up fighting a battle that we were never made for.

Genesis 4:1-15 gives us a good example of that. Cain and Abel were brothers, and Cain was very jealous of Abel because of his better offerings to the Lord. The Bible doesn't state why his offerings were better. However, we know that in Proverbs 21:27 it says, *"The sacrifice of an evil person is detestable, especially when it is offered with wrong motives."* Perhaps he had wrong motives and his intentions weren't right. God examines both our motives and the quality of what we offer him. When we give to God and others, we should have a joyful heart because of what we are able to give. We should not worry about how much we are giving of our time, money, possessions, and talents, for all things are God's in the first place.

One day, out of retaliation, bitterness, and anger, Cain killed Abel. What were the repercussions of that decision? He was a homeless wanderer of the earth (Genesis 4:12). Cain killed Abel because of jealousy and discontentment. No one told him to do it, but it was out of discontent in his heart that he did.

Another example is Joseph and his brothers in Genesis 37:3-20. After Joseph told his brothers about the vision God gave him of them bowing down to him, they were jealous because they didn't want their brother ruling over them. This shows us that if we are not secure in our identity, purpose, and relationship with God, we will begin to compare our journey with the journeys of others. Because they were jealous, they threw Joseph in a pit and sold him into slavery. But God's will prevailed. They still bowed down to him, and Joseph ended up saving their lives.

God's plan has a purpose. You never know what God has in store for you or for someone else. Instead of envying someone for the good God is doing in their lives, rejoice with them. Celebrate the purpose God has given them, and keep in mind that He is probably working something much greater than you can understand right now. You never know when or if God will put them in a position that could involve helping you or someone else in the future.

Fear is the opposite of faith. How can we combat it? We can fight against our fears by renewing our minds in the Word and the things of God.

"Don't copy the behavior and customs of this world, but let God transform you into a new person by changing the way you think. Then you will learn to know God's will for you, which is good and pleasing and perfect." - Romans 12:2

This is done by meditating on the Word, consistently studying it, and letting it guide and validate your life. Allow the words from the Bible to sink in and become your thoughts. Apply them to the way you walk through your life. It all starts in the heart. As stated previously, Proverbs 23:7 KJV says, *"For as he thinketh in his heart, so is he."*

If we don't combat fear, it can keep us from becoming what God created us to be and from fulfilling our purpose in life.

God's Timing

Scripture tells us that there is a season for every activity under the heavens (Ecclesiastes 3:1). There is a time and season for our weather: summer, fall, winter, and spring. The trees and flowers are in full bloom in the summer, when fall hits they start to dry up for the cold of winter, and when spring comes back around we start to see blooms again. God provides for the plants and animals during each season. There is a time for it all. He is never a day late, and He is the redeemer of time. He will provide for us during each season of our lives. We should appreciate our portion now before expecting God to give us the next.

"He replied, 'The Father alone has the authority to set those dates and times, and they are not for you to know.'" – Acts 1:7

The disciples had so many questions for Jesus. He provided some answers for them, but He also expressed that there were some things they simply were not supposed to know. Allowing them to know the dates and times of His plans could very well have prevented them from seeking God in the meantime. Jesus wanted them to know that God has ultimate authority over time and that trusting in that would allow them to come to a much greater faith in Him than knowledge of fates ever could.

Imagine that God laid out your life for you. Imagine He allowed you to know the dates you would graduate, get married, launch your career, and have your first child. Would you still seek Him?

"God has made everything beautiful for its own time. He has planted eternity in the human heart, but even so, people cannot see the whole scope of God's work from beginning to end." – Ecclesiastes 3:11

When it states that God has *"planted eternity in the human heart,"* this means that we can never be completely satisfied with earthly pleasures and pursuits. We are created in God's image, and our ultimate thirst is a spiritual one. We have eternal value. Nothing but the eternal God can truly satisfy us. We can't find satisfaction through social media, television, Internet, jobs, or human relationships. He has built us for a restless yearning for a perfect world that can only be found in His perfect rule. He has given us a glimpse of the perfection of His creation. But it is only a glimpse. We cannot see into the future or comprehend everything that has happened, is happening, and has yet to happen. So we must trust God and do His work on earth with what He has given us now, while resting in His love and promises.

Trust in the Lord

"Your name, LORD, endures forever,
your renown, LORD, through all generations.
For the LORD will vindicate his people
and have compassion on his servants.
The idols of the nations are silver and gold,
made by human hands.
They have mouths, but cannot speak,
eyes, but cannot see.
They have ears, but cannot hear,
nor is there breath in their mouths.
Those who make them will be like them,
and so will all who trust in them.
All you Israelites, praise the LORD;
house of Aaron, praise the LORD;
house of Levi, praise the LORD;
you who fear him, praise the LORD.
Praise be to the LORD from Zion,
to him who dwells in Jerusalem.
Praise the LORD." – Psalm 135:13-21 NIV

If your prayers don't seem to be getting answered, you may be tempted to stop trusting the Lord and start chasing other "gods." Trusting in Him at all times may start to seem "old fashioned" or useless. But, as the scripture above states, *"Your name, Lord, endures forever, your renown, LORD, through all generations"* (v. 13).

His name never goes out of date, and this includes His promises, sovereignty, protection, plans, and love for us.

The above scripture also tells us that we become like that in which we put our trust. If you put your trust in the "gods" of silver and gold, money, or fame and fortune, then you will become like them – spiritless, lifeless, blind, and deaf (v. 16-18). If you trust in God, you will be filled with life and joy as you become like Him.

Keep trusting God, *"For the Lord will vindicate his people and have compassion on his servants"* (v. 14). Hence, the psalmist calls the people of God to praise and fear the Lord (v.19-21).

You need to remain totally dependent on God and look for Him to vindicate you. When things aren't working out as you wish, be patient. Stop trying to move ahead of God. His timing is perfect. Trust Him.

Chapter 2

Celebrate Your Age

Getting back to the vision boards many of us have for our lives, you may have a ton of plans made as you approach your "milestone" age. Maybe you want to be married, to have kids, to have a million dollars in the bank, or to know you found Mr. Right. That's the American dream, right?

But whose dream was this anyway, and where did it come from? Why are we trying to live up to someone else's dreams or expectations? What happened to the belief that God knows what is best for us? He is the Creator of all things and chose us in such a special way that He knew the numbers of hairs on our heads (Luke 12:7). This applies to all of us, not just married people with kids.

As the title of this book suggests, I'm 30, I don't have any of those things, and I'm at peace.

That peace came from spending time with the Lord and knowing His Word. I believe what it says, and I believe the Lord means what He says, too. Spending time with Him led me to start comparing my life to the people in the Bible instead of those in this world. As I seek Him first above everything, God has given me peace that surpasses all understanding and wisdom. What keeps me in that place, despite the pressures I feel from family and society, is knowing that God is in control. Through seeing His protection and covering throughout my entire life, I know His promises are true and that He only wants the best for me. I am privileged and grateful for each season I am in, as I know each season has its purpose and will prepare me for the next.

Many people fear reaching this age, or another one, because they start to think about what they don't have or where they wish they were in life. Maybe you feel as if you don't have a purpose or that you're not living in your purpose. Maybe you're waiting on God's promises to come to fruition. Whatever the reason for your fear may be, I want you to know that **God's timing is not always our timing. At the right time, God has a way of taking the world's idea of perfection and blowing it right out of the water with His promises for your life.** So although I don't have all those things that I mentioned before, I am expectant and excited to see what my Heavenly Father is preparing me for.

If you need someone to compare your life to, look toward the people in the Bible. There are many examples that will edify you in whatever season you are in. As I was approaching 30, I realized this age is actually a significant age in the Bible and that it demonstrates the impossible being made possible through God's authority.

Here are some examples of this:

• **Jesus officially started His ministry at 30:** *"Now Jesus himself was about thirty years old when he began his ministry. He was the son, so it was thought, of Joseph."* - Luke 3:23

• **David became King at 30:** *"David was thirty years old when he began to reign, and he reigned forty years in all."* - 2 Samuel 5:4

- **Joseph stepped out of his wilderness season and became second to Pharaoh at 30:** *"And Joseph was thirty years old when he stood before Pharaoh king of Egypt. And Joseph went out from the presence of Pharaoh, and went throughout all the land of Egypt."* - Genesis 41:46 KJV

- **Ezekiel was called by God as a prophet at age 30:** *"Now it came to pass in the thirtieth year, in the fourth month, in the fifth day of the month, as I was among the captives by the river of Chebar, that the heavens were opened, and I saw visions of God."* - Ezekiel 1:1 KJV

- **John the Baptist was 30 when he came out from the wilderness to pave the way for the Messiah (Jesus):** We know John was roughly 30 because the Bible says he was born six months before Jesus, and Jesus started his ministry at age 30 (Luke 1:5-33).

These important leaders and figures from the Bible stepped into their purpose at 30. As you can see, we should be celebrating the significance of growing into our destinies as we go through life. We shouldn't be sulking about what we haven't achieved by a certain time while trying desperately to figure out what's next. Let your hope be in the Word and in God's promises, not in the world and its compromises.

At the same time, this isn't an excuse to sit around and do nothing. Although these leaders stepped into their purpose at this age, they had been preparing to hear from and do for God long before that.

Jesus Started His Ministry at 30

What was Jesus doing before God used him?

Before God used Him, Jesus had been a carpenter since the age of 12 (Mark 6:3).

How had he prepared?

Jesus prepared by being about His father's business. He fasted and kept a close knit of friends around Him. Through His preparation, He grew in wisdom, stature, and favor with God and man (Luke 2:52).

What were his character traits at 30?

At 30, He was honest, bold, and honorable. He didn't conform to the world, and He was determined to fulfill all that God called Him to (John 4:34).

David Became King at 30

What was David doing before God used him?

He worked for his father as a keeper of sheep. He was disregarded by his family because of his birth position – the youngest of eight sons. God called and anointed David as he was out keeping the sheep (1 Samuel 16:8-11).

Don't underestimate what God is teaching you in the environment you're in, even if it feels unimportant or insignificant at times. David was anointed when he was out keeping sheep. He was anointed to become king over Israel. But he wasn't king right away. He served Saul, who was the king until he was appointed. Before those milestones, David was busy working in the field, at his post. He didn't miss out on anything because he was in position. He was ready when someone was sent to anoint him as king. So, we don't have to put ourselves in certain places to get what we think God has in store for us. We don't have to lie, cheat, or dishonor God. God will find you and anoint you to do what He has called you to do. Just stay in position and be obedient to Him. This shows us that when we are faithful in the little things, God honors us with more.

How had David prepared?

Keeping the sheep meant he had time to think. David spent a lot of time looking over the sheep and looking at the glory of what God made. God built in him a heart to sing about His glory in all creation (Psalm 8, 19:1-4). Keeping the sheep took a special heart and special care. Those who were assigned to this position knew how the sheep needed the care and help of a good shepherd. In the same way, God is our shepherd and we are the sheep of His pasture (Psalm 100:3). During those years, God built in David a heart that would sing about the Lord as his shepherd (Psalm 23).

Keeping the sheep also meant the shepherds had to trust God in the midst of danger. David had lions and bears to contend with, and the sheep had to be protected (1 Samuel 17:34). During this time of tending the sheep, he killed animals who were after the sheep. This practice of killing the animals equipped and actually trained him to go up against one of his greatest rivals, Goliath. David killed Goliath as a young boy, and he was prepared for it because he had been in practice while tending the sheep.

David's years of keeping the sheep were not waiting time; they were training time. David was a great man and a great king over Israel because he never lost his shepherd's heart.

Psalm 78:70-72 NIV speaks of the connection between David the king and David the shepherd: "*He chose David His servant and took him from the sheep pens; from tending the sheep He brought him to be the shepherd of his people Jacob, of Israel His inheritance. And David shepherded them with integrity of heart; with skillful hands he led them.*"

David was a shepherd, but there were a lot of shepherds. David was good looking (1 Samuel 17:42), but so were a lot of young men. Let's see why God placed favor over David in the next point.

What were his character traits at 30?

God described what made David special in 1 Samuel 13:14 NIV: "*The Lord has sought out a man after His own heart and appointed him ruler of His people.*"

What made David special was that he was a man after God's own heart. God's choice of David shows us that we don't have to quit our jobs and enter into full-time ministry to be people after God's own heart. We don't need to be famous or prominent to be people after God's own heart. We don't have to be admired or even liked to be people after God's own heart. We don't need status, influence, power, the respect and approval of men, or great responsibilities to be people after God's own heart.

Where did David get this heart?

David got this heart from time spent with the Lord. First and foremost, David wanted to have and was seeking a pure and authentic relationship with God. He wrote:

"The Lord is my shepherd, I shall not want ..."
- (Psalm 23:1 KJV)
"The Lord is my light and my salvation-- whom shall I fear? ..." -
(Psalm 27:1 NIV)
"I lift up my eyes to the mountains - where does my help come? My help comes from the Lord, the Maker of heaven and earth ..." - (Psalm 121:1-2 NIV)

Joseph Stepped out of His Wilderness Season at 30

What was he doing before?

Before God used Joseph, he was tending the flocks. At the age of 17, God gave him a vision that the land would be bowing down to him and that he would rise to a position of leadership over his parents and brothers (Gen 37:5-11). From this, Joseph knew and believed that God had destined him for greatness. From his point of view, these dreams were evidence of divine blessing and not of his own ambition.

However, his brothers viewed it differently. They saw his dreams as further manifestation of the unfair privilege that Joseph held as the favorite son of their father (Gen. 37:3-4). Joseph wasn't anyone of importance or influence at the time. His family wasn't royalty. He was just an average person despised by his brothers because he had favor. So his brothers plotted murder against him. When that didn't succeed, they sold him into slavery.

Maybe God has given you a specific dream or vision that some people in your life disagree with or don't understand. Don't be discouraged. God called *you* to do it, not them. Know that anything the enemy means for harm, God can always turn around for your good.

How had Joseph prepared?

When Joseph was sold into slavery, he served in the master's house under Potiphar, an officer of Pharaoh. He could've easily fallen into depression and self-pity. Instead, he gave his all in the season he was in and worked unto the Lord. If you're in a season that you don't understand or in which you can't see God's promises being fulfilled, know that each season connects to the next. Give your all where you are presently. This shows and builds your character, faith, and relationship with God.

Joseph was faithful and competent in his position of serving in Potiphar's house. He was so competent, in fact, that he was promoted to be his master's personal steward. Potiphar *"put him in charge of all that he had"* (Gen 39:4).

Then, Joseph was tested with temptations from Potiphar's deceitful and promiscuous wife. She tried to lure him to sleep with her, but he fled from the temptation (Genesis 39:6-10).

"So Potiphar gave Joseph complete administrative responsibility over everything he owned. With Joseph there, he didn't worry about a thing – except what kind of food to eat! Joseph was a very handsome and well-built young man, and Potiphar's wife soon began to look at him lustfully. 'Come and sleep with me,' she demanded. But Joseph refused. 'Look,' he told her, 'My master trusts me with everything in His entire household. No one here has more authority than I do. He has held

back nothing from me except you, because you are his wife. How could I do such a wicked thing? It would be a great sin against God.' She kept putting pressure on Joseph day after day, but he refused to sleep with her, and he kept out of her way as much as possible."

Although he did that, Potiphar's wife still accused him of sleeping with her. It was absolutely false, but Joseph was put in prison because of this accusation. While in prison, he would interpret the dreams of the other prisoners. The guards took heed of this. When the king needed a dream deciphered, they summoned Joseph to interpret the dream because no one else in all of the land could. When Joseph interpreted the dream, he said it meant that they would have seven years of surplus and seven years of famine. He said the dream also gave the logistics of what they should do during that time. Potiphar was grateful because Joseph saved the nation with his interpretation when no one else could. He was so grateful, in fact, that he wanted everyone to serve the God that Joseph served and make Joseph king over Egypt.

Joseph provides such a strong model in showing us that even when we are falsely accused or wrongly treated, we can and should still carry on with the work God has given us, allowing and trusting Him to make it right in the end.

How did God make it right at the end of Joseph's story? How did God bring it all together for Joseph's good and for His glory? God made Joseph ruler over Egypt. His brothers and father had to bow down to Him. However, it was during a season where he was imprisoned that his interpretation of dreams was the key God used to lead him out. If he had succumbed to the opinions of those around him and shrunk back each time someone defiled him, he would not be where he was at that time. Each season, no matter how vile it seems, has purpose. God has a calling for it that is beyond your comprehension or understanding. Know that there will be a time when people will see the fruit of your calling and anointing, even if they didn't believe you or see it at the beginning.

What were his character traits at 30?

At 30, Joseph led the nation and followed the instruction in the dream the Lord gave him. He forgave his family and those who did him wrong. This was significant to his character, because it could have been extremely easy to hold those grudges and not let them feast on the food or give them what they needed to survive during the famine. He was a leader of integrity, wisdom, and discernment in tough times. Pharaoh characterized him as "*discerning and wise*" (Genesis 41:39). These characteristics enabled him to do the work of strategic planning and administration as he managed the food crisis. His character of reconciliation shined through as he was loyal to and forgiving of his family, even when they were guilty. Joseph could have taken the advantage he had as a ruler and gotten back at them, but instead he gave them the advantage.

How many of us would relinquish the opportunity of revenge even when we were "right?" That is God's responsibility, not ours (Romans 12:19).

Ezekiel Was Called by God as a Prophet at Age 30

What was he doing before?

Ezekiel served as a Jewish "street preacher" for twenty-two years. Imagine how much patience and trust that took. How many of us could remain in the same place for twenty-two years without getting restless and questioning God?

How had he prepared?

Ezekiel prepared during those twenty-two years of training as a priest before God called him as a prophet (Ezekiel 2:3). As a street preacher, he told everyone about God's judgement and salvation and called them to repent and obey. He literally lived what he preached, as God asked him to illustrate his messages with dramatic object lessons (Ezekiel 4-5).

What were his character traits at 30?

Ezekiel received vivid visions and delivered powerful messages (Ezekiel 3:10-11). He served as God's messenger during Israel's captivity in Babylon. This was significant to his character because it can be challenging to speak to those who have hardened their hearts to God. He became a tough and courageous man so he could reach a hard and stubborn

43

people (Ezekiel 3:8). Through his story, we learn that even the repeated failures of His people will not prevent God's plan for the world from being fulfilled. Each person's response determines his or her eternal destiny. God has people through whom He can work, even in seemingly hopeless situations.

John the Baptist was 30 When He Came Out from the Wilderness to Pave the Way for the Messiah (Jesus)

What was he doing before?

According to Matthew 3, John the Baptist was a prophet. However, before this, he was tucked away with God in the wilderness preparing the way for Jesus. You may think "Okay, what kind of life is this?" He sounds like a peasant or an unsuccessful person. But our obedience to God, no matter what it looks like, has a greater purpose and understanding than we know. God uses each season for His purposes and glory. For the Lord says in Matthew 11:11:

"I tell you the truth, of all who has ever lived, none is greater than John the Baptist. Yes, even the least person in the kingdom of heaven is greater than he is! And from the time John the Baptist began preaching until now, the kingdom of heaven has been forcefully advancing."

How did he prepare?

John lived a simple life as he focused on the kingdom set before him. It is written that he wore clothes made out of camel's hair with a leather belt around his waist. His diet was also a simple one of locusts and wild honey (Matthew 3:4).

John's ministry grew in popularity. As recounted in Matthew 3:5-6, *"People went out to him from Jerusalem and all Judea and the whole region of the Jordan. Confessing their sins, they were baptized by him in the Jordan River."* We also see that he spoke very boldly to the religious leaders of the day, the Pharisees and the Sadducees, calling them a "brood of vipers" and warning them not to rely on their Jewish lineage for salvation, but to repent and *"bear fruit in keeping with repentance"* (Matthew 3:7-10). People of that day simply did not address leaders, religious or otherwise, in this manner out of fear of punishment. But John's faith made him fearless in the face of opposition.

What were his character traits at 30?

God appointed John as the messenger to announce the arrival of Jesus. He was a fearless confronter, uncompromising, and known for his remarkable lifestyle of blind devotion and utter surrender to Jesus and His kingdom. He was *"one voice in the wilderness"* as he proclaimed the coming of the Messiah (John 1:23). He was a man filled with faith and a role model who wished to share his faith with others. Although he was a well-known preacher who attracted large crowds, he was content for Jesus to take the higher place. In John 3:28 ESV he says, *"You yourselves bear me witness, that I said, 'I am not the Christ, but I have been sent before Him.'"*

When you are content to do what God wants you to do and let Jesus be honored for it, God will do great things through you. Through these examples, we must resist the temptation to jump ahead before God. Don't jump ahead. Trust His timing.

Age Ain't Nothing but a Number

These stories are great examples of how God's timing and plans for our lives often don't line up with the expectations of the world. It's much bigger than just feeling good about being 30, or whatever your "milestone" age is. Yes, these people stepped into their calling at 30. However, if they weren't obedient in their seasons of preparation and expectant about how God would use them, God wouldn't have used them at that time. Age is pretty insignificant through all of this. **It's purely about contentment in Jesus and how He is developing you spiritually.**

So, what did I do on my 30th birthday? I was on a plane leaving from Cape Town, South Africa, and heading to America. No, it wasn't for vacation. I was actually leaving the place that had been my home for the last three years and transitioning back to Atlanta, Georgia, the place God was sending me for my next season.

Before I left, many people were saying, "Wow, you're flying on your birthday? That's too bad!" Well, no, actually it wasn't. It was a significant time for me. It was an honor to fly on my birthday because it represented how I was glorifying God through stepping into a new season, age, and destination He was calling me to. I wasn't just traveling; I was stepping out in faith. I left my life, friends, job, and church family to walk into the unknown. I didn't know what the next season held for me, but I knew the One who held it in His hands. I wouldn't have changed that day for anything.

Leading up to my 30th, I did a daily video countdown to celebrate. Why? I was putting myself out there without the world's care. I was celebrating the courage to step into the unknown by faith alone. I didn't know exactly where I was going or how I would get there, but I just trusted God and He carried me through it all.

I knew someone who locked themselves in their room and didn't leave their house on their 30th birthday because they felt they were not where they wanted to be. That's not okay. Remember, age doesn't determine specific milestones for success. **True success is walking in God's will for your life, and that is at any age!**

We have to be close to and in tune with God to know whether or not we are walking in His will. Just like spending time with your friends and family enables you to know them better, you will get to know God more deeply and fully as you continue to seek Him (Jeremiah 29:13). In His timing, He will give you the peace and conviction to go step into your calling and chase after His plans for your life. As it states in Matthew 6:33, everything will fall into place and all you need will be added unto you when you first seek Him and His Kingdom.

Our birthdays should be a celebration of another year of walking in God's plans, a spiritual check to see if what we are doing lines up with what God has asked us to do. Rejoice in knowing that you are protected, loved, and guided by the Most High, Jesus Christ. I don't know what the future holds, but I'm taking it day by day. It's the peace that surpasses all understanding that confirms that I am in the right place.

How are you celebrating your next birthday? What areas do you need to grow in? As we are living and serving unto Him, let's rejoice in knowing that He doesn't make mistakes.

"'For I know the plans I have for you,' declares the Lord, 'plans to prosper you and not to harm you, plans to give you hope and a future.'" – Jeremiah 29:11 NIV

"Have I not commanded you? Be strong and courageous. Do not be afraid; do not be discouraged, for the Lord your God will be with you where you go."
– Joshua 1:9 NIV

"Do not be anxious about anything, but in every situation, by prayer and petition, with thanksgiving, present your requests to God. And the peace of God, which transcends all understanding, will guard your hearts and your minds in Christ Jesus." – Philippians 4:6-7 NIV

Chapter 3

What Does It Mean To Be Content?

Society often makes us feel like we can only be content when everything is working out for us, when life is together and progressing in the way that it "should" be. Maybe contentment to you is when you feel like you've accomplished everything you've wanted — graduating, finding a man, getting married, and having children — within a certain timeframe. After that, you can truly rest and enter into contentment.

Contentment shouldn't be based on an event, a person, an award, or an accolade. It can't be measured by whether or not you have a man in your life. It can't be measured by how much money you have in your savings account or the number of square feet in your house. The Holman Bible Dictionary defines contentment as, "An internal satisfaction, which does not demand changes in external circumstances."

Based on that definition, can you say that you are a content Christian today? Do you have an internal satisfaction that cannot be changed based on the worldly things you may or may not acquire?

*"But godliness with **contentment** is great gain. For we brought nothing into the world, and we can take nothing out of it. But if we have food and clothing, we will be content with that." –1 Timothy 6:6-8 KJV*

Contentment means that you are focused on the eternal and you are aware of the shortness of life. Your life is committed to seeking first the Kingdom of God, the only thing that will last. Since you trust in the sovereign Lord, you're not tossed around by changing circumstances or pressures the world may try to throw at you.

For example, the world may try to tempt you with the ladder of career success. If you won't be content until you reach a certain step on that ladder, you need to realize that your ladder is on the wrong wall – the wall of worldly things. Having an eternal perspective means placing your contentment in God, His plans, and His definition of success for your life. Contentment is being free from greed and anxiety. It means removing circumstances as the basis for happiness.

Contentment in God is constantly tested by the trials of life. You may not have everything you want when you want it, but remember that you have what you need in God. You can be confident in the will of God's plan for you and unshaken by the world. When you are content, your attention is not divided or double-minded because of your circumstances. God tells us to seek the kingdom first, above all things, and He will give us everything we need (Matthew 6:33).

What do you want most out of life? What do you spend most of your time thinking about? If you spend more time thinking about how you're going to find a husband than you spend thinking about how you are meant to establish God's kingdom here on earth, that's a sign that you are seeking contentment in the wrong areas. His glory and how you're meant to make Him known should be your heartbeat if you are seeking His kingdom above all else.

Is It a Sin Not to Be Content?

It is sinful to be discontent because you are literally telling God that He is not enough for you and that you are not satisfied in the season that you are in. God wants you to be a successful single, not a coping single.

The apostle Paul provides us with an excellent example of what it means to show contentment in challenging situations. He was put in prison for teaching about Jesus, but he still continued his ministry work from within his cell. He wrote approximately one third of the chapters in the New Testament, some of which were written by him to the early churches while he was imprisoned.

Paul had so much taken from him, but he had the Lord and that was enough. You cannot buy the peace and contentment that the Holy Spirit gives. Paul didn't have a lot. He even had a physical ailment. We could probably give him a pass to throw himself a pity party, but what he says in his letter to the Philippians is an incredible statement of faith, contentment, and trust in God.

*"I rejoiced greatly in the Lord that at last you renewed your concern for me. Indeed, you were concerned, but you had no opportunity to show it. I am not saying this because I am in need, for I have learned to be **content***

whatever the circumstances. I know what it is to have plenty. I have learned the secret of being **content** in any and every situation, whether well fed or hungry, whether living in plenty or want. I can do all things through Christ who gives me strength." - Philippians 4:10 -13 NIV

The last verse, "I can do all things through Christ..." is the key! He will give you the strength to be content throughout each season and circumstance.

Maybe you're reading this thinking that you already have all the material things you could want: a nice house, expensive clothes, and a fancy car. However, all of that can be taken away in a moment's notice. Unless your contentment is based on eternal principles and values, it will not last. If your main concerns lie in the things of this world, your life will be a rollercoaster.

Contentment comes from making godliness our priority and from placing value in eternal things, not in temporal or worldly things. You can't keep the things you gain in this world, but you can keep the reward you gain from the Lord.

My Story

I didn't come from a storybook home. My parents got divorced while I was in the sixth grade, but I haven't let that stop me. Your upbringing or past don't have to define you and your story. If your parents got divorced or if you didn't have a godly example of a relationship growing up, that doesn't have to be your reality.

I believed in God at a very young age and was quite aware of His presence and Spirit. Although I didn't know Him on the same level as I do now, I always felt He had a special covering and protection over my life.

My first supernatural experience with the Holy Spirit occurred when my father passed away. I was a daddy's girl, and he died from cancer just days before my college graduation. The moment I received the news through a phone call from my sister, I could see angels surrounding me, hugging me. It was my first time experiencing peace that was unexplainable, a peace that truly surpasses all understanding. This gave me a new revelation of God as my heavenly father.

God told me that my first relationship would be with my future husband. I know you may be thinking, "Wait, what? You don't want to explore your options? How do you know that they will be 'the one?'" In short, I've always trusted that God knew what was best for me. I had a sense of security and peace that the one God had for me would come in His timing.

I've never been in love, or even close to it. When I was in high school and college, I would think to myself, "I'm not going to marry this person, so why date them?"

Although I thought like this, no one else I knew felt the same way or showed those same actions of contentment. I always felt insecure in my reasoning because all the people around me had boyfriends and were going on dates each weekend. It almost seemed as if you had a disease if you weren't dating.

This was especially true for me in college. People were concerned that I was still single. When I spent time with my girlfriends, they would often start talking about their boyfriends and ask me questions about why I didn't have one or if I was looking for one. But I felt peace in spending time with my family, hosting gatherings at my home, and cooking for friends. Dating was not on my radar.

I would often ask God if something was wrong with me because I never had the urgency or desire to go out on dates. I always felt that when that season came, He would stir up that desire in me. I actually went out with guys to fit in because everyone else was doing it, but I never had peace about it. While I was busy trying to fit in with the world, what I didn't realize was that God had set me apart for a reason.

"Don't copy the behavior and customs of this world, but let God transform you into a new person by changing the way

you think. Then you will learn to know God's will for you, which is good and pleasing and perfect." – Romans 12:2

It wasn't until after graduating from college, moving to New York City, then moving to Dubai that I started to develop a real relationship with Jesus for myself. I grew up in a Christian home, but the Bible was never talked about verbally around the dinner table. Yes, we said grace, but that was about as far as our conversations with God went.

While living in Dubai, seven thousand miles away from home and my church family, I missed that fellowship and time with other believers. One of my friends introduced me to the New Living Translation Bible. As I began reading that version of the Word, it was like the words were jumping out of the pages and into my heart. My heart was soaking in each word. After beginning to read the Word for myself, my friend and her husband began to disciple me. Through this process, I came to realize how important it was to know the Word for myself.

As I started to read the Bible, I also began comparing my life to the people I was reading about. This is when I fully realized that God had a protection over me. I knew I didn't have to go out with a guy, fall in love with him, have it end horribly, and get my heart broken just to know that they weren't right for me. It's fine to be single. In fact, the apostle Paul said he wished everyone was single just as he was, so that they could devote all of their time to pleasing God (1 Corinthians 7:7).

Nothing was wrong with me. I was normal. My contentment was a gift from God.

> *"I want you to be free from the concerns of this life. An unmarried man can spend his time doing the Lord's work and thinking how to please him. But a married man has to think about earthy responsibilities and how to please his wife. His interests are divided. In the same way, a woman who is no longer married or has never been married can be devoted to the Lord and holy in body and in spirit. But a married woman, has to think about her earthly responsibilities and how to please her husband. I am saying this for your benefit, not to place restrictions on you. I want you to do whatever will help you serve the Lord best, with as few distractions as possible."* – 1 Corinthians 7:32-35

Even if you don't naturally have the gift of contentment in singleness that Paul speaks of in the Bible, the Holy Spirit can help you. You can ask Him for the gift. In James 4:2, it states, *"You don't have what you want because you do not ask God for it."* The Lord isn't sitting up in Heaven withholding it from you. He can give it you if you ask with the right heart.

Regardless of what your background is or what you may have done in your past, you can be content in Jesus. It's vital to develop this mindset. Without Christ, you can't be truly content.

I'm so happy that I didn't get married when I was in high school or college, or even several years after that. I've since realized that the type of guys that I was attracted to earlier in life mirrored my relationship with Christ; neither were at their fullest potential. God knew I wasn't ready. The timing wasn't right. Before, the things I paid attention to were simply whether or not a guy was polite, funny, or made me smile. He didn't even necessarily have to be a Christian. But that's all surface-level stuff. There is a purpose in marriage; it's a ministry, and God says very clearly in His Word, *"Do not be unequally yoked with unbelievers"* (2 Corinthians 6:14).

I now know, based on scripture, what I am looking for in a spouse. If they aren't saved and if God isn't first place in their life, ***I'm not interested.*** I don't care if they have six-pack abs, six cars, or a six-figure income. I don't have time for someone who isn't all-in with God, and you don't either. I want someone who leads my house with authority from the Lord, who loves me like He loves Christ, who hears from God, and who is not afraid to live out the God-ordained calling on his life.

That being said, I truthfully don't care if I never get married. I'm so content with where I am now because of the love and peace that I already have in Christ. Being single and spending time with my Jesus is all right with me. Being in relationship with Him has led me to live on three different continents and travel to more than thirty-six countries. Life with Jesus is seriously a dream. He is my comforter, provider, King, and best friend.

Since He told me that I will one day be married, I'm using this time now to prepare myself to be the best helpmeet I can be (Genesis 2:18). This is part of what serving, spending time with God, and developing in the fruits of the spirit is being used for. I will never get this quality time back. I know when I am married, I'm going to have many responsibilities that will divide my time between my wifely duties and my quiet time with Jesus.

Singleness isn't a disease or a curse. It's a calling. So many people act as if I'm lacking something when I tell them I'm still single, as if I won't step fully into my calling until I'm married. If this happens to you, don't allow those words to discourage or distract you. You have a God-led assignment and a purpose where you are right now, and you don't want to miss out on that because you're too worried about finding a husband. God leading me to write this book is an example of how He's using me in my single season.

Rejoice in your singleness because you have that much more time to grow in your faith, learn from and spend time with God, and truly fall in love with Him. If you aren't allowing God to build your foundation now when you're single, what would make Him want to bring someone else into the equation that will take up all your attention? He is a jealous God, and He loves you so much (Exodus 34:14).

Be content with where God has you right now. Ask Him how He wants to use you during this season. Focus on growing in your relationship with Him. The leaders discussed in the previous chapter embodied this. They were focused on their assignment. They wanted to honor and glorify God in all that they did. If you live your life this way, God will bring the right person to you in **His perfect time.**

"Each of you should continue to live in whatever situation the Lord has placed you, and remain as you were when God first called you. This is my rule for all the churches." – 1 Corinthians 7:17

"To everything there is a season, and a time to every purpose under the heaven." - Ecclesiastes 3:1 KJV

*"I am not saying this because I am in need, for I have learned to be **content** whatever the circumstances."*
- Philippians 4:11 NIV

Chapter 4

Identity

Just as our true contentment should be found in Christ, so should our identity. It is important to be grounded in this, as society often suggests that our identity is wrapped up in material things or status. Who we are is not based on our skin color, the car that we drive, the clothes that we wear, the job that we have, the degrees we attain, or whether or not we are married. Our identity is in Jesus Christ and in Him alone.

The best compliment that someone can give me is that they see Christ in me; not that my hair is slayed, my shoe game is strong, or that my outfit is cute. It's nice to hear those things, sure, but it doesn't get better than hearing that someone can see God's love and beauty through me. This is because I know where my true worth is found.

He is our creator. He is the potter, and we are the clay (Isaiah 64:8). Before you know who you are, you have to know whose you are. As a believer, the answer is that we belong to Jesus Christ.

"Before I formed you in the womb I knew you, before you were born I set you apart; I appointed you as a prophet to the nations." - Jeremiah 1:4-5 NIV

"So God created human beings in His own image. In the image of God, He created them; male and female he created them." - Genesis 1:27

As the above scripture states, we are made in His image. God created us. He created us to be His and to walk in fellowship with Him. He will equip you, train you, and develop and mature you to be who He has called you to be.

> *"I praise you because I am fearfully and wonderfully made; your works are wonderful; I know that full well. My frame was not hidden from you when I was made in the secret place, when I was woven together in the depths of the earth. Your eyes saw my unformed body; all the days ordained for me were written in your book before one of them came to be."* - Psalm 139:14 -16 NIV

God formed you before you were born. You have biological parents, of course, but God himself fashioned you and knit you together in your mother's womb. This verse testifies that the personal relationship between God and His child takes place in the womb, or even earlier. We do not choose God before God chooses us.

> *"You did not choose me,"* Jesus said to his disciples, *"but I chose you and appointed you to go and bear fruit."* – John 15:16 NIV

> *"Praise be to God and Father of our Lord Jesus Christ, who has blessed us in the heavenly realms with every spiritual blessing in Christ. For he chose us in him before the creation of the world to be holy and blameless in his sight."* – Ephesians 1:3-4 NIV

This promise is for the whole church. Therefore, it is for the comfort of every Christian. God not only knows you, but He also chose you; and He did so long before you were ever conceived.

Every Christian has a calling. There is a general call, of course, to believe in Jesus Christ. But everyone who believes in Christ also has a special calling to a particular sphere of obedience and ministry.

"I knew you before you before formed you in your mother's womb. Before you were born I set you apart and appointed you as my prophet to the nations."
– Jeremiah 1:5

As we can see in Jeremiah 1:5, before Jeremiah was born, God already had a purpose for him. Think of an invention, such as a washer and dryer. Before someone could make it, they would to have a purpose and a need for it. In order to know the purpose and how it would work, you would have to read the inventors instruction manual so that you would use it properly. You wouldn't use the washing machine to store your groceries in. Its use would be to wash clothes. If you used it for any other purpose, you would then be misusing the machine and not using it to its fullest potential.

Jeremiah had a mission to accomplish and a message to deliver to his generation. We may not all be called to be prophets, but there is a particular calling on all of our lives that requires our immediate obedience.

Let's take a look at a few single women in the Bible and how we can learn from their examples and mistakes. We'll also look at a married woman and a widowed woman who were content in their seasons and callings despite the unordinary position that they were called into. It doesn't matter what our relationship status is, contentment needs to follow you no matter the season.

MARY AND MARTHA

(Luke 10:38-42)

Mary and Martha were sisters. Both of them were single, but their personalities were complete opposites. Martha was a go-getter, a people pleaser. Mary, on the other hand, was content to listen to Jesus speak. Understandably, Martha was a bit upset at her sister's lack of help with preparing the meal for their guests. She went and asked Jesus to get Mary to help. Jesus' response is classic: *"Mary had chosen the better of the two"* (Luke 10:42).

Martha was so worried about the preparations and the fancies of the dinner, but Mary realized that there was no need to worry because Jesus was right there. The quality of the dishes and the serving of the food was all just extra. Mary chose the better of the two by taking the opportunity to enjoy Jesus' presence.

It is very easy to become like Martha and always be concerned about the technical aspects within a project or ministry. Those things are important, but they are crumbs compared to the meat of the gospel. Have you become distracted with the things of this world? Are you getting too caught up in the outer preparations instead of taking the time to actually be present? Have you become hung up on the color and the type of fabric of the curtains? Or, are you willing to be changed by the power of God's Word? This is all part of understanding your identity in Christ and your true purpose in fulfilling God's will for your life. The choice is yours.

THE WIDOW WITH THE TWO MITES

(LUKE 21:1-4)

The widow in this story was very poor and had only two coins to her name. This was hardly enough to provide for herself, yet she gave all that she had to the Lord. Though the world would have deemed her offering as less than the others, Jesus said she put in more because it was all she had (Luke 21:4). This woman truly lived by faith, not by sight (2 Corinthians 5:7).

She could have come up with a million reasons to keep the money. I'm sure she had a lot of expenses or things she needed to buy in order to survive. But out of faith, she chose to give all that she had, knowing God would provide for her needs. This shows that she had great confidence in her identity, worth, and purpose in Christ.

As single women, we may sometimes find ourselves facing difficult times. We might struggle with our finances, our emotions, our health, or other challenges that seem to overwhelm us and keep us from giving our all to God. In every situation, we have a choice. We can freely give of our money, time, and talents to God while relying on and trusting in Him, or we can struggle with unbelief, hoard what we have, and place our worth in those things.

RUTH

(RUTH 1-4)

Ruth was a single widow and served her mother-in-law Naomi, who was also a widow. As singles, we can be selfish with our time, but Ruth was not. She availed it to Naomi and said, *"Wherever you go I will go; wherever you live, I will live"* (Ruth 1:16).This was done without expecting anything in return. Ruth didn't even live in the same land as Naomi, and she moved just so she could take care of her. She could have been comfortable where she was, but she didn't let familiarity hold her in one place. On top of that, Naomi was a bitter woman. Can you imagine willingly moving your life to serve a woman with that disposition? But Ruth needed nothing from Naomi. She gave the advantage and God found favor with her.

While she was serving her mother-in-law, she worked the fields of Boaz, a well-known and respected man. Ruth wasn't checking for Boaz. She was minding her own business and just gathering food for Naomi. Boaz soon sent for Ruth because he had an attraction to her and wanted to pursue her. They soon got married, but marriage had not been her focus. Serving God and fulfilling the assignment that was in front of her was her focus.

How many of us try to jump ahead of God instead of focusing on the task at hand? We do not have to put ourselves out there for people to notice us or pursue us. Our assignment is just enough to be satisfied. It is easy to become distracted in life, but just know that there is purpose where you are. God needs your focus. He is aligning everything around you to move as you obey Him.

We may even have leaders that are tough to work with. Ruth didn't run from this challenge. God develops you in these situations. If there is something that you feel needs to be added to your life, God will shift that in due time.

DEBORAH

(JUDGES 4)

When I first read and understood the story and significance of Deborah, it was a profound moment. God used this woman because the present leader, Barak, couldn't step up to the plate. The people of Israel had been oppressed for twenty years. Deborah, a woman, led the charge, which was unheard of at the time. Deborah was a prophet. She shared with Barak the plans that God had for their battle in the war. Barak didn't want to do it alone, so he asked Deborah to join him.

If Deborah wouldn't have been content in who she was and of God's power, she might have backed away. But she believed more in God's power and direction than in her own ability. She got her strategy from God because she had an intimate relationship with Him. He was her source. She also gave credit to Him for the victory, not herself. She could have easily taken the credit, as the wisdom and direction she gave in defeating this battle worked. However, she pointed everything to God. Through this, others gave glory to God and served Him.

Deborah was just a prophet judging Israel at the time, but in a matter of seconds, became a leader of the nation. Are you in position and available to do what God is asking of you? Deborah's life shows us the significance in being available. Don't be hesitant. If God can't use you, He will certainly use someone else. His will is going to be done, no matter what. And when He does use you, all glory must go to Him. It is easy for us to want to get recognition for achievement and a job well done, but we must point others to Christ and His power. None of our efforts are done in our own strength, but in Him and HIM alone.

PROVERBS 31 WOMAN

(PROVERBS 31)

You may have heard about the Proverbs 31 woman, as she is a very popular biblical figure. What was most significant about her is that, first, she was a virtuous woman. Oxford Dictionary defines virtuous as "having or showing high moral standards." This is exemplified by our character and can be displayed at any age and throughout any season of life. Her strength and dignity do not come from her achievements, looks, or any materialistic accumulation, but only from her reverence for God.

As singles, we should exemplify the characteristics of the Proverbs 31 woman unto the Lord as though He is our husband (Isaiah 54:5). We shouldn't do this in "practice" for whoever the Lord brings. We are not completing these things in anticipation of what will come because we can never define God's timing.

Before we can enter into any relationship, we need to know our identity and our value. Before we are a wife, a sister, a mother, or a friend, we are disciples of Jesus Christ. That should be our first identity. That is what defines us.

The standard that we should hold ourselves to when it comes to relationships and friendships is that of God. We should be searching for Godly examples and Christ-like people that will hold us accountable to God's will and plan for us and encourage us in our walk with Him. If we start to lose sight of this, we run the risk of lowering our standards and entering into relationships we weren't ever meant to have.

Your pathway to true identity and contentment can only be found in Him and through His strength and guidance. Ask Him to help you be a more Christ-like single woman, and He will begin to shape your heart.

Chapter 5

The Wait

I don't think there are many people out there who would say they enjoy waiting. Whether we're waiting to go to the doctor or waiting on the phone for hours to talk to someone from our cell phone company, waiting is never really fun, right? When we think about "waiting" for our spouse, an ideal job, or another dream or goal we have in mind, it might seem like we're in a constant period of waiting.

Maybe it's time we start looking at this from a different perspective. Are we ever really waiting, or are we in purpose? To wait on something insinuates that we are doing something to pass the time until it happens. But what if what we are doing during that time is actually what God has called us to? If we are living in God's calling, we shouldn't be focused on waiting for things that may or may not come in the future. We should be truly present in and focused on where He has us now.

I've heard people say that they are waiting until they get married to do certain things with their lives. We shouldn't be thinking this way, relying on a future that might not come for five or ten years down the road. We don't know when it will come or if it will at all, and we shouldn't be holding off on our dreams and plans until it does. If we do, we'll be missing out on so much precious time right now.

Go on that international trip with your family or your girlfriends. Don't wait to make it a couple's trip. Work toward buying that house or car you've always been dreaming of! You don't have to wait for a man to do that either.

We shouldn't be waiting on a spouse. We should be walking in purpose, in position, and on mission to wake up daily and do what God is asking us to do in both the big and the small things.

Singleness is more than a season. Singleness is a calling.

Don't think for a second that you can only be used by God when you're married or when you've reached a certain age. Jeremiah was only 20 when he was sent out to be a prophet among the nations. Age, background, wealth, popularity, and relationship status don't define our glory. What defines it is our obedience to Him in all things.

We are never truly waiting because we are in purpose. What does it look like to be in purpose? We all have unique gifts and callings that God has made us for.

Who gives these gifts? The Holy Spirit (1 Corinthians 12:1). Each of the gifts that the Holy Spirt gives you equips you for your individual purpose and callings.

The following is a verse that encourages us in these gifts:

"In his grace, God has given us different gifts for doing certain things well. So if God has given you the ability to prophesy, speak out with as much faith as God has given you. If your gift is serving others, serve them well. If you are a teacher, teach well. If your gift is to encourage others, be encouraging. If it is giving, give generously. If God has given you leadership ability,

take the responsibility seriously. And if you have a gift for showing kindness to others, do it gladly." – Romans 12: 6-8

It may be easy for us to take credit for all of these gifts that God has given us. However, we must not boast in ourselves or about what we can do because every gift that we have is from God and is purposed to bring glory to Him (James 1:17).

It's also important for us not to sit on those gifts, as the following verse implies:

"Each of you should use whatever gift you have received to serve others, as faithful stewards of God's grace in its various forms." – 1 Peter 4:10 NIV

Maybe God has given you a broad vision and a specific task to complete. Maybe for you it's obeying God in the last thing He told you to and trusting that He will show you the rest of the plans in His timing. For me, it's just waking up and obeying God in the day that's before me.

Aside from our unique gifts and callings, our universal purpose in Christ is sharing the good news, making disciples, and being a servant to the kingdom. This is important. When sharing the good news, you are spreading the message of the gospel and making disciples by equipping others to pick up their cross and follow Jesus. Being a servant to the kingdom is carrying out the work and will of God throughout the earth and being the hands of feet of Jesus.

Some people might think that you have to be a "pastor" to be in ministry, but God's work comes in all shapes and sizes. You don't have to be anyone of "importance." We are all vessels and part of the body, and none of our roles are higher than the others. In fact, they are of equal importance. We all must be in position, fulfilling our purpose. Others are relying on and are affected by our obedience.

> "Just as a body, though one, has many parts, but all its many parts form one body, so it is with Christ. For we were all baptized by one Spirit so as to form one body — whether Jews or Gentiles, slave or free — and we were all given the one Spirit to drink. Even so the body is not made up of one part but of many.
>
> Now if the foot should say, 'Because I am not a hand, I do not belong to the body,' it would not for that reason stop being part of the body. And if the ear should say, 'Because I am not an eye, I do not belong to the body,' it would not for that reason stop being part of the body. If the whole body were an eye, where would the sense of hearing be? If the whole body were an ear, where would the sense of smell be? But in fact God has placed the parts in the body, every one of them, just as he wanted them to be. If they were all

one part, where would the body be? As it is, there are many parts, but one body.

The eye cannot say to the hand, 'I don't need you!' And the head cannot say to the feet, 'I don't need you!' On the contrary, those parts of the body that seem to be weaker are indispensable, and the parts that we think are less honorable we treat with special honor. And the parts that are unpresentable are treated with special modesty, while our presentable parts need no special treatment. But God has put the body together, giving greater honor to the parts that lacked it, so that there should be no division in the body, but that its parts should have equal concern for each other. If one part suffers, every part suffers with it; if one part is honored, every part rejoices with it.

Now you are the body of Christ, and each one of you is a part of it." – 1 Corinthians 12:12-27 NIV

Let's explore each of these areas of our universal purpose as mentioned above and see how we can be living them out during our single seasons.

Sharing the Good News

This is done by sharing the message of the gospel and testimonies of God's goodness to those around us - at work, at a coffee shop, in our family, anywhere!

For the Lord tells us in Mark 16:15, *"Go into all the world and preach the good news to everyone."*

We're often quick to tell people about the exciting events in our lives such as an upcoming sale, our favorite singer coming to town, or who the next president is going to be. Why? They can be easier to talk about. We're not ashamed of these things or worried about what others will think. But when it comes to sharing Christ, it can be easy to let ourselves back away out of fear, an insecurity of some kind, or shame. I want to encourage you not to be ashamed of the gospel of Jesus Christ.

Romans 1:16 NIV states, *"For I am not ashamed of the gospel, because it is the power of God that brings salvation to everyone who believes: first to the Jew, then to the Gentile."*

Just like Paul, you can choose to be unashamed. As disciples of Jesus Christ, it's our responsibility to share the good news. There are so many ways that this can be done. It will look differently for each of us, as we're all called and led to do God's work in unique ways.

I want to share with you a little bit about how God has called me to serve and spread His good news around the world. For three years, I lived in Dubai and worked as a flight attendant with an international airline. It quickly became much more than a job. The Lord exposed me to so many things through traveling and seeing the world. For example, I twice had the opportunity to volunteer at orphanages. Instead of using my vacation time to go to Spain or Italy, I would research communities in need across various continents, volunteer for them, fundraise for their communities, speak to them about Jesus, encourage them, and help instill values in their local communities. I didn't see this as a sacrifice. Ministry work became my desire and passion, and God soon opened the door for me to do it fulltime.

If you feel like your job doesn't provide opportunities to ministry work, you can still minister to others through your actions. You don't even have to say a word about Christ.

Jesus tells us that people will know we are His disciples by the way that we love one another (John 13:34-35). People will notice how you treat them and the way you respond to them. Your integrity and your character will be evident. Something will be different about you, and people will take notice. Let your light shine.

Never underestimate your season or position. Don't limit where God has you. I'm constantly asked where I get my joy from, and the answer is that it comes from an opportunity to share about my contentment in Christ.

Making Disciples

The Lord says to *"Go and make disciples of all nations, baptizing them in the name of the Father and the Son and the Holy Spirit."* – Matthew 28:19

To make disciples means we are making followers of Jesus. This is our responsibility. It is also a sacrifice, as Jesus stated to his disciples in Matthew 16:24:

"If any of you wants to be my follower, you must turn from your selfish ways, take up your cross, and follow me."

When we are making disciples, we're teaching others about Jesus and His ways and imitating His actions. The way that we live our lives out on a daily basis is a big part of this. What are our lives speaking and demonstrating to others?

Our fruits of the spirit (character traits) speak louder than words. As Christians, we are known by our fruit (Matthew 7:16). These fruits are love, joy, peace, patience, kindness, goodness, and faithfulness (Galatians 5:22). If you saw an apple tree and someone told you that it was an orange tree, you wouldn't believe them because you would see apples hanging from it, right?

The same thing applies when you mentor others and teach them about Jesus Christ. If you say that you are a Christian and love God, then your actions need to align with who God calls us to be through scripture. People are checking that your fruit (kindness, gentleness, patience, etc.) matches what you are talking about. Living by the fruits of the spirit will emulate the God that is inside of you. You do not want to deter people to the wrong way of living by showcasing something that is not fruitful while still attaching the Christian name to it. Which fruits are you showcasing? Which fruits should you be working to further develop?

Living by the fruits of the spirit will encourage, inspire, and challenge people to seek God. For example, let's say you're going through a trial right now because you just got laid off from your job and don't have any leads for a new one. God has given you peace that surpasses all understanding so that, through this situation, you are still able to carry on, rest in Him as your provider, and trust that He will open up the right doors in His timing. He is caring for all of your needs and is working behind the scenes on your behalf. You trust Him. Meanwhile, someone else could be going through a similar situation, but they are feeling depressed and hopeless because they don't know what to do. They are in bondage to worry and fear. They have become anxious in the present, which is distracting them and causing them to go off course in several areas of their life. They come across you, with a smile on your face and peace in your heart. When they see that, they will want to know how in the world you are able to have peace in such a trying time. This is an opportunity for you to share Jesus. Even if they don't understand, your example has planted a seed, and God will make it grow (1 Corinthians 3:6).

It's also important that we do not point people to ourselves as we are teaching them about Jesus and being walking examples. This can breed pride, and we don't want others to value the messenger more than the message. We should point them to Christ. Paul wrote this letter to the church and its leaders in 1 Corinthians 3:5:

"After all, who is Apollos? Who is Paul? We are only God's servants through whom you believed the good news. Each of us did the work the Lord gave us."

At the time, they were looking at the leaders as "gods." But we are purely messengers. Instead of the names of Paul and Apollos, enter your name. We are all just God's servants fulfilling His assignment on this earth. Although there is sacrifice as mentioned before, God graces us and protects us through it all.

Making disciples doesn't mean you have to sit in church all day while reading the Bible and teaching someone the ways of God. It can involve volunteering at a school during the day, helping out at an afterschool program, blogging about your Christian walk, starting a prayer group, or leading a Bible study. There are so many options!

I did a two-year internship in Cape Town, South Africa, with an international ministry. I worked with their nonprofit foundation doing community work, building churches, and teaching young moms through an early childhood development program. I spent a lot of time with those I had the opportunity to disciple. This was a significant part of Jesus' ministry, as He spent a lot of time fellowshipping with and mentoring His twelve disciples.

In all of this, don't get caught up in the idea of making someone a "perfect Christian." Remember that no one is perfect, including yourself. Jesus was let down by the people He discipled, including Judas and Peter, and He forgave them (Luke 22). Don't give up if someone you disciple makes a mistake or goes back to their old ways. Pray for them. Continue to walk alongside them and encourage them. God is the only one who can change and grow someone's heart. You are doing your part by planting the seed. God will do the rest.

Being a Servant to the Kingdom

Being a servant to the kingdom means following God as He leads you, no matter the cost.

"Then Jesus said to his disciples, 'Whoever wants to be my disciple must deny themselves and take up their cross and follow me.'" – Matthew 16:24 NIV

The leaders in the Bible we discussed earlier didn't just one day "arrive" at their calling. They were preparing during their wait. Jesus was in the synagogue praying and fasting. Joseph was in jail, rejected and lied to. You might think that God had forgotten about him. I mean, God had given him a dream that he was supposed to be a ruler. Those seasons of hardship sure didn't seem to equate to God's calling for him, but He had something incredible in store up the road.

If people are telling you that your past or your present don't line up with what God has promised, know that God fulfills His promises, redeems, and has purpose for each situation you are in. Good or bad, He takes what the enemy means for harm and turns it around for our good (Romans 8:28).

God often uses the people you would least expect for big assignments so that He receives an even greater amount of glory.

For example, David was average. He wasn't a man of royalty or high education. Still, he was faithful in keeping the sheep and working for his father when God called him to be king and slay Goliath (1 Samuel 17).

Both John and Ezekiel lived a simple life. John was a street preacher before God called him to something new. Little did he know, he was training for the assignment God would entrust him with next, which was making the way for the Messiah. Jesus praised John as a prophet, saying there was none who were greater (Matthew 11:7-11).

The same applies to Ezekiel. He lived a simple life and only wanted to glorify God. He was a prophet that restored a nation from dried bones, a nation that God told Ezekiel to encourage to follow Him, a nation that was in the path of destruction. It was hard for him, but the Lord told him that if he did not tell everyone he was sent to about the punishment for not following God, he would be held accountable for the blood of those who died in their sins (Ezekiel 33:8-9).

None of these men were just sitting at home eating fried chicken and Cheetos while sipping on lemonade and waiting to hear the Lord speak to them. They were proactive. They moved when God called them to. They were obedient and faithful to Him with a pure heart. As they stepped out and followed Him, God moved right along with them. He was always with them.

The same thing applies to us. We are in training and on mission. Each season prepares us for the next, and only God knows what that next season will be. Let's do our part and give our all where we are now so we will be fully equipped when we enter into whatever God has next for us.

Chapter 6

Are You Looking For Your Other Half?

First of all, we shouldn't be looking. In the Word it says, "**He** who **finds** a wife finds a good thing and finds favor from the Lord" (Proverbs 18:22 ESV). Secondly, we are whole and complete in Christ: "And in Him you have been made **complete**, and He is the head over all rule and authority" (Colossians 2:10 NASB).

The world tries to convince us that we won't be whole until we have a big savings account, the latest fashions, and the flashiest car parked along a white picket fence. Those things don't make you complete. They'll only make you want more. They may have been ingrained in your mind as "must haves" since your childhood or be all that you know as important, so we constantly have to renew our minds in this area.

2 Corinthians 10:5 NIV says, "We demolish arguments and every pretension that sets itself up against the knowledge of God, and we take captive every thought to make it obedient to Christ." It doesn't say that your parents will do it, it doesn't say that your teacher will do it, and it doesn't say that your siblings will do it – you have to do it intentionally. Capture those thoughts and make them obedient to Christ, not to the ways of the world.

"But I'm looking for my better half, my other half."

"I'm not complete until I'm married."

Maybe you hear those phrases a lot, and maybe you're in that state of mind right now. Maybe you feel lost. Are you looking for someone to complete you, to make you whole? If you do not rely on God and seek Him for your needs while you're single, you will always rely on humans to fill voids only God can fill. You cannot put your entire life into someone who is not perfect. They will fail you. If a perfect and holy God cannot please you, a husband never will. You need to be whole before you entertain bringing someone else in. Two halves make two halves, and I don't know about you, but I don't want a half-baked Adam.

What qualities does the man you're interested in possess? Yes, he can *look* good, but *is* he good? Looks will only get you so far. I remember liking a guy in college, and I thought he was so fine. I soon realized that what looked good on the outside was not pure on the inside. His intentions were not to be in a relationship but to be undercover friends with benefits, and I'm not talking about getting me a discount at a store.

This experience showed me that not all that glitters is gold. He was dealing with insecurities that he was trying to mask to get women to like him. He was using my kindness as a bait to get what he wanted. This made me realize that what I "want" is not necessarily what I need. It showed me that I was dealing with the sin of lust. I didn't know about him or who he was as a person. I was just infatuated with his looks and the idea of him. It also gave me a sour taste in my mouth and showed me how important it is not to go ahead of God, but to trust Him.

I'm so thankful that the Lord led me to break it off with this person. At that time, I couldn't articulate that I wanted to stop talking to him, so I would create scenarios that would make him upset and want to leave. For example, sometimes I would talk to another guy right in front of him. Yes, I know that is kind of petty, but I honestly couldn't muster up the confidence to stand on my own and articulate that this wasn't a healthy relationship. I thank God for giving me His grace in this area.

Imagine what I could have been doing in place of spending time with him, talking to him for hours on the phone, or thinking about him. I could have been spending time with the Lord, focusing on my calling and purpose, doing my homework, or participating in other much more productive things. I was caught up in a distraction, and I can't take that time back. I encourage you to remember this next time you're tempted to pursue anything that isn't in line with God's will. When the Lord says no, He is trying to protect you.

Do You Find Yourself Getting Tired

of Doing Life on Your Own?

When you grow and develop in your relationship with God, He gives you rest. You're able to get to know Him as your provider. He will give you advice, guide your steps, give you comfort and peace, and fill all your voids. God is the source, not man.

You have to be spiritually strong and know your identity in Him before entering into a relationship. When you do get married, you two are supposed to work together as a team. The Bible mentions in Ecclesiastes 4:9-12 that two is better than one.

The two of you will be more equipped to accomplish the will of God if you are working together rather than alone. For example, you two could bounce ideas off each other, balance each other out in terms of strengths and weaknesses, or tag team when it comes to sharing God's Word. This will reap a harvest of good things that will bring God glory.

The Lord says in Genesis 2:18 NIV, *"It is not good for the man to be alone. I will make a helper suitable for him."*

A helpmeet is someone who comes alongside a person with the purpose of helping them fulfill the mission that God has given them. How can you uplift him, help him, and encourage him when you don't know the authority you have in Christ? For example, he could be having a bad day or be tempted to give up on a business pursuit that God gave him the vision for. If you are strong in your relationship with God, you could remind him that the Lord will finish the work in him that He has started. You could tell him that in his weakness God will give him the strength. You could encourage him that we must trust His timing and not give up or grow weary when doing good. However, if you have a spirit of worry and haven't combated that, you could become a burden and cause him even more distress.

In addition, your husband should add to your anointing. The purpose of marriage is for people to come together to fulfill a mission. Being focused on the mission is what will bring your family together. Matthew 6:31-33 states, *"So don't worry about these things, saying, 'What will we eat? What will we drink? What will we wear?' These things dominate the thoughts of unbelievers, but your heavenly Father already knows all your needs. Seek the Kingdom of God above all else, and live righteously, and he will give you everything you need."* Like the scripture states, if you seek the kingdom first, then everything will be added to you.

To give an example of this outside of the context of marriage, have you ever been on a short-term missions trip before? Think about the people that you went with. Were those the people you would usually hang out with? Not necessarily, perhaps. But what happens at the end of the trip? You start to miss the people who were there with you - from the old lady to the young kid. By the end of it, you became the best of friends with people of all different ages, races, cultures, and backgrounds.

When I went on a missions trip to Mozambique with my church, we were all from different backgrounds and of varying ages. Still, we formed relationships with one another seamlessly and still keep in touch to this day. This is because we were all coming together under one mission to fulfill one thing. Our eyes and hearts were set on the prize to fulfill this mission. We didn't have time for arguments – they weren't even on our minds. We all loved each other and had the best time. Even language barriers didn't obstruct that.

Before going on the trip, we didn't have to practice being nice to one another. We didn't come together and say, "Okay, let's be tight at the end of this trip." As we were on the trip, we found ourselves aligning together as we all sought the kingdom of God first. We were living out our lives and our relationships through love.

Love is the thread that holds everything together. Our love will stand out amongst all else. For the Lord said, *"Your love for one another will prove to the world that you are my disciples"* (John 13:35). He is not just talking about loving someone when they treat you well or when they give you a gift. He is speaking of unconditional love, the same love that He gives and shows us.

"Love is patient, love is kind. It does not envy, it does not boast, it is not proud. It does not dishonor others, it is not self-seeking, it is not easily angered, it keeps no record of wrongs. Love does not delight in evil but rejoices with truth. It always protects, always trusts, always hopes, always perseveres." – 1 Corinthians 13:4-7 NIV

You see, love is a verb. Therefore, there should be some love-like actions that follow when we apply this definition to our lives. This shows the world that we are different and that we belong to Him. Choosing not to argue and fight is the gospel. Forgiving one another is the gospel. Giving the advantage is the gospel. Making sacrifices for others showcases the gospel. When you have a family that is focused on serving the Lord and not the world, that's the gospel. Showing God's ordained purpose in marriage in the flesh is the gospel.

The Significance of Marriage as a Ministry

Let's dive a little deeper into what marriage looks like as a ministry. Ephesians 5:21- 22 NIV says, *"Submit to one another out of reverence for Christ. Wives, submit yourselves to your own husbands as you do to the Lord."*

When you see the word "submit" in our day in age, it is often perverted to mean slave. But when you are submitting, you are under the mission. You are submitting to the mission you have as a family and as a couple. Many women struggle with this because they do not trust their spouse. But if you marry a godly man who has the Holy Spirit living within him and plenty of spiritual fruit evident in his life, you can have confidence in honoring and trusting him as a husband and as a leader.

No one is perfect, of course, but if you can't trust him or if you have second thoughts about him while you are dating, don't think that he will change when you are married. The only person who has the authority and power to change someone is Christ, as He makes us all into a new creation when we accept Him as our Lord and Savior (2 Corinthians 5:17).

Don't be tempted to make a bad relationship work by saying, "Well, I can make him saved." You want your future husband to have his own natural convictions from God. That is how he will be able to lead you properly. Ephesians 5 breaks this down.

Is he going to a Bible study each week because he's with you and you told him to, or is he going out of his own desire? What is his relationship like with the Lord on his own? It's important to remember that just sitting in church each week and serving on one of the teams does not make someone a Christian. You can sit in a garage, but that doesn't make you a car.

I'll give you an example of this. At a mega church I used to go to, there was a guy I was interested in. I thought he was a godly man. When he began making advances, I thought it was too good to be true. I mean, he quoted scriptures in our conversations and everything. Well, I soon found out that he was ENGAGED to another mutual friend of mine at the same church. I couldn't believe it. I sensed in my spirit that something wasn't right all along, but I was trying to push it off because I didn't want to believe it. I mean, he was a leader in church, so I wanted to believe that made it okay. It is incredibly important to check them by their fruit and listen to those promptings from the Holy Spirit when the Lord is trying to warn you.

These promptings from God can go both ways. We must obey Him when he tells us to do something, as well as when He tells us not to. Whenever you go against your convictions, you're opening a door that the Lord ordered to remain shut. And you will bear the burden of everything that flows through that open door. The Lord wants to cover you, but He also gives you the power of choice.

Going back to Ephesians 5:21, a significant part of this verse is, *"Wives, submit yourselves to your own husbands as you do the Lord."* If you doubt what God tells you and you don't obey Him in the little things, then that spirit of control will carry on into your marriage as well. If you have a hard time obeying God, how will you be able to align with your husband? This is a parallel comparison. As you are in line with Christ, it will be so much easier to submit to your husband's authority as head of the household.

As the scripture continues in verse 23, *"For the husband is the head of the wife as Christ is the head of the church, his body, of which he is the savior. Now as the church submits to Christ, so also wives should submit to their husbands in everything."*

I don't know about you, but I see this as a relief. Men have a huge responsibility to lead the home, and we are called to submit. What an honor it is for us to be led and know that our faith-filled husbands will guide us. I find so much peace in that, and I look forward to when that time comes for me. Find comfort in the Lord, and He will give you peace in this too.

The scripture continues in verses 25-33:

> *"Husbands, love your wives, just as Christ loved the church and gave himself up for her to make her holy,*

cleansing her by the washing with water through the word, and to present her to himself as a radiant church, without stain or wrinkle or any other blemish, but holy and blameless. In the same way, husbands ought to love their wives as their own bodies. He who loves his wife loves himself.

After all, no one ever hated their own body, but they feed and cared for their body, just as Christ does the church - for we are members of his body. For this reason a man will leave his father and mother and be united to his wife, and the two will become one flesh. This is a profound mystery – but I am talking about Christ and the church. However, each one of you, also must love his wife as he loves himself, and the wife must respect her husband."

The part of the verse that states, *"cleansing her by the washing with water through the word,"* means that a husband is a spiritual leader to his wife and teaches her the Word of God. He is the spiritual leader because He is guiding her in faith and in God's Word. Most importantly, it means that he is an example of what it looks like to live out the Word of God.

When you are married, your focus will be split between serving your husband, spending time with God, and taking care of your home. Nothing is wrong with that at all, but serving your husband must be done from a place of strength and confidence in your identity as a woman of God.

Proverbs 31 Woman

Going back to the Proverbs 31 wife, this passage is filled with so much wisdom and fruit. It would take forever to break down each verse and share its significance, but I'm going to highlight a few.

I love this verse: *"She is clothed with strength and dignity, and she laughs without fear of the future"* (Proverbs 31:25).

What is your spiritual clothing; what do you wear? Do you wear the title of girlfriend, or do you carry yourself like a wife? You shouldn't wait to become a wife to start acting like one. You should show those characteristics beforehand, as they give us a description of what it means to be a godly woman. She does not fear the future, but she laughs from her belly with joy because of God's faithfulness and promises over her life. Do you plan to do this only when married? I don't think so! You should have this embedded in you now. It should be your lifestyle and should come from a place of authenticity. The same goes for any relationship you are in. You attract what you carry.

You wouldn't want to go swimming with a life jacket that was flat and would only fill up once it hit the water, would you? No, you would want to see the fruit of it first before making that commitment to go into the deep end.

"Her children arise and call her blessed; her husband also, and he praises her." – Proverbs 31:28 NIV

What is it about your life and the way you live that glorifies God? This is what will attract and inspire your husband and family. Don't just wait or think those qualities will appear by osmosis when you say, "I do." Start now.

"She considers a field and buys it; out of her earnings she plants a vineyard." – Proverbs 31:16 NIV

You see the word "considers?" She doesn't take on something new without seriously considering it. She doesn't just put something into her life without peace.

"Charm is deceptive and beauty is fleeting; but a woman who fears the Lord is to be praised." – Proverbs 31:30 NIV

Deceptive charm means batting your eyes, talking smooth, and dressing fancy to get your way. Stop being on the prowl for a man and start being on the ball for the things of Christ. Your foundation shouldn't be in MAC cosmetics, but in His Word.

Standing Firm in Your Purpose before the Ring

Do you feel like you are ready for marriage now and find yourself praying to God each day to just hurry up already? He is not a genie bottle, where you can just rub Him the right way and expect Him to give you everything you want. Are you not content and secure without a man by your side?

Like I mentioned earlier, you cannot be fulfilled by an imperfect, earthly man if you cannot first be fulfilled by a perfect, living God. Again, you don't want to depend on your husband for your joy and security. He can't be your everything. You will deplete him. You want to empower him with confidence and security. Your prayer should be that God won't bring him until you are both ready. You don't want to squander His calling, and vice-versa.

If you are content in Christ and know your identity in Him, then when you enter into a relationship, no one will be able to steer you away or manipulate you to do things contrary to what God called you to do. There will be distractions, of course, but those will not shake you because of the confidence and contentment you have in Him.

A good friend of mine once entered into a relationship with the wrong person. Let's take look at her story and the lessons she learned from it.

My friend knew her purpose and calling from God before starting this relationship. The Lord had revealed to her that she was going to have a world-wide women's ministry and preach around the world. But the guy she was dating at the time told her that she was living in a fantasy and that those were unrealistic dreams. He wanted to be a politician and needed someone by his side that looked "worldly smart." He said that type of job wasn't enough or wasn't "successful" in his eyes.

So, by his influence, she put herself in grad school to pursue and study a degree that she wasn't even passionate about and that didn't align with what God had revealed to her. She quit school after the first semester, and she quit that relationship as well. She had come to realize that she needed to remove those things from her life and get back in line with God's plans.

Shortly after, she met the man who is now her husband. On their first date, she shared what she felt like the Lord called her to do, and his response was, "Good, me too." Now she is walking in her calling and God has anointed her for this ministry alongside her husband. But if she would have entertained and continued in that previous relationship, she definitely would not be where she is today.

Do you see how imperative it is to seek God before and when choosing our spouse? It is so much more than six-pack abs and great teeth. As my friend's example illustrates, entire lives and destinies can be shaped by this decision.

Don't Shrink Back

There might be many instances where others try to shake your faith and make you break when it comes to trusting God with your spouse, whether it be your colleagues at work, family members, friends, or other acquaintances. But do not give up or give in to them. Take heed to this scripture:

"So do not throw away your confidence; it will be richly rewarded.

You need to persevere so that when you have done the will of God, you will receive what he has promised.

For,

"In just a little while,
he who is coming will come
and will not delay."[

And,

"But my righteous one will live by faith.
And I take no pleasure
in the one who shrinks back."[

But we do not belong to those who shrink back and are destroyed, but to those who have faith and are saved. –
Hebrews 10:35-39 NIV

This verse tells us not to throw away our confidence, as mentioned previously. Do not grow weary in doing good. Find security in following His will. You will reap a harvest in due time. In verse 36, it states that you need to persevere to receive what He has promised. You see, the Lord fulfills His promises. He will do His part, but we must do ours. This requires us to be patient and make sure that we don't rush and run ahead of His will. In verse 37, it states He is coming – Jesus is returning. As no one knows the day nor the hour, our focus should always be about Him and for Him.

The scripture continues in verse 38 to state that His righteous one will live by faith. Do you remember what faith means from our earlier discussion? Faith is the assurance of things hoped for and the confidence of things unseen (Hebrews 11:1). This means having confidence that God will bring everything you need in each season in His timing.

What sticks out to me is the last part of verse 38, *"and I take no pleasure in the one who shrinks back."* I love it. We have to understand that God dares us not to shrink back. He is not pleased when we shrink back, whether we shrink back from where we are going or what God is calling us to because we are in the wrong relationship, because we didn't wait, or because we didn't live by faith. We have a distinct guideline.

God says to live by faith, to be righteous, and not to dare to shrink back.

This doesn't just apply when things are easy. It applies especially when people lie to you, when others deceive you, and when everyone thinks you're crazy.

"You Christians, you are nuts to wait. I can't wait for that long, I need someone today." Does that sound familiar? If you are Spirit-led, then you are doing what you are supposed to do regardless of what others say. It is so important that you understand this and that you develop, mature, and strengthen your muscles in your confidence in God. In every season that you are in, you will need it. You can't jump to Train C if you need to be on Train A. It's a process. If you are led by the Spirit and pursue God, you will not be deceived.

Attacks from the Enemy

Let's be real for a moment. Attacks will come. During those attacks, the enemy is after your mindset. If he is able to get a hold of that, this will then affect your marriage, your other relationships, your career, and your calling. You're currently a threat to him because he sees what you can be and do in order to increase the kingdom of God. When you don't know who you are and WHOSE you are, the enemy will try and feed you lies that have the potential to destroy.

For example, I love this analogy about ketchup that my friend shared with me. Someone asked her if she kept her ketchup in the fridge or on the counter. She said, "In the fridge." The lady then proceeded to ask her, "Why do restaurants keep them on the counter?" This caused my friend a bit of confusion, and she started to doubt if she should keep her ketchup in the fridge. She began to question it. Later, she researched it and found out that it is indeed meant to be in the fridge. This same thing happens to us when we doubt what God has called us to do or who He desires us to be. Many people around you could be doing different things or saying you should do something a certain way, but when you are strong in your relationship with God, you will know what He is speaking to you. Don't doubt Him or become double minded.

The Definition of Holiness

When you share your standards with others, they might think that you are "holier than thou" for living the lifestyle that you do, but you can't scale holiness. Holiness is a heart condition.

Ephesians 4:22 NIV states, *"You were taught, with regard to your former way of life, to put off your old self, which is being corrupted by its deceitful desires; to be made new in the attitude of your minds; and to put on the new self, created to be like God in true righteousness and holiness."*

As imperfect and sinful humans, many of our desires are deceitful. Your goodness is not contingent upon whether or not you have a husband, the best car, a six-figure income, or the latest wardrobe. It's contingent upon His goodness, and He is good all the time. The enemy will always try to distract you by placing deceitful desires in your heart that don't align with the Word of God.

What is leading you? If it isn't the voice of God, then what is it? What is guiding you when you make decisions? There is only one true Spirit that leads and guides us. If it's not God, then it's not good.

Galatians 5:16 states, *"So I say, let the Holy Spirit guide your lives. Then you won't be doing what your sinful nature craves."*

For example, let's look back in Genesis 4 where we see Cain and Abel. They were two brothers who were born into sin after their parents Adam and Eve ate from the forbidden apple tree. Cain craved to be the center of attention and look good in front of God. He had a root of offense and pride in his heart. They both gave an offering to the Lord, but He looked down on Cain and showed favor to Abel. This was because Abel gave with a pure heart and Cain gave with ulterior motives.

"Then the Lord said to Cain, 'Why are you angry? Why is your face downcast? If you do what is right, will you not be accepted? But if you do not do what is right, sin is crouching at your door; it desires to have you, but you must rule over it.'"
– Genesis 4:6-7 NIV

The Lord told Cain that he better master that thing. We can overcome sin not because we are "holier than thou," but because God said that we can do it.

Cain brought his sacrifice and tried to do all of these things above and beyond to impress God, but Abel was the one who was faithful and just brought what he had. God didn't find favor in Abel's sacrifice, but in his heart.

As you can see, holiness is a heart condition. We are holy when we say, "God, I am going to honor You above all things." Holiness doesn't mean that we are better than anyone else, but it does mean that we are set apart. We have been transformed by the renewing of our minds. To pursue holiness means to flee from things not of God.

As single women, we should be pursuing the things of God. Do not get discouraged when attacks come. Know that when they do, you are usually on the right path. People like to live in the sin that they are in, and your lifestyle may contradict or convict them. They may feel uncomfortable, but it is important to love others and not deliberately offend them or think we have to defend ourselves. Let your life do the talking, and the fruit of it will speak for itself.

As we pursue the things of God, we will be complete in Him, not lacking any good thing.

Chapter 7

Pressure from Family and Friends

Imagine it's nearing the end of the year and the holidays are about to roll through. First, it's Thanksgiving. Then, it's Christmas. You're sitting around the table and everyone is asking you where your man is, why you aren't married, and where their grandkids are. Maybe you don't even have to imagine this. Perhaps it's already happened to you on at least one occasion.

Or maybe its Valentine's Day and you have no valentine to spend the evening with. Do you feel like you have to rush and find someone just for this holiday? Don't. You can take yourself out. If you see people out on dates and start to feel badly that you aren't doing the same, don't fall into the trap of asking, "Why me?" Instead, thank God for protecting you and saving you for the right one in the right timing.

Or maybe your mom is telling you to get pregnant because she wants a grandchild and that she will help take care of the baby. There might be generational curses present if someone is trying to pressure you into wanting to do things out of order so soon. A generational curse is bondage from sin that has been passed down from one generation to another. The Bible tells us that the sin of the parents can cause the same pollution to be handed down to their children:

"Our fathers sinned, and are no more; and we have borne their inequities."— Lamentations 5:7 ESV

Although we can be born into it, we can decide whether we will continue in the sin or take the way out. You can choose to be the end of the very pattern that has been hovering over your family for generations.

"You shall not bow down to them or worship them; for I, the Lord your God, am a jealous God, punishing the children for the sin of the parents to the third and fourth generation of those who hate me." – Exodus 20:5-6 NIV

The Lord does forgive us for our sins, but sins that are intentional can have a stronghold on you that will plant seeds and continue on for generations to come.

"I lavish unfailing love to a thousand generations. I forgive iniquity, rebellion, and sin. But I do not excuse the guilty. I lay the sins of the parents upon their children and grandchildren; the entire family is affected —even children in the third and fourth generations." - Exodus 34:7

How does it continue?

Children see what their parents do and often emulate those actions. If a parent doesn't deal with their sin, it gets passed on and children become heirs of the issues. What the older and wiser men and women do not teach, the younger generation will not know.

Sin is punishable by death. The reward of sin is death. The sin of Adam and Eve is what we deal with today. It's not something that we have to teach. It's innate in us. That is the reason we have to be born again. Sin requires payment. This payment is what Jesus did for us on the cross.

If you struggle with the same bondages as your parents or see your siblings with the same problems, then it's quite possible that you are suffering from the effects of a generational curse. The good news is that the blood of Jesus is more powerful than any bondage that may have been handed down to you. You can be set free and released from the effects of any generational curses.

Don't let your family's insecurities rub off on you. You have a choice, and it can end with you. If you jump ahead of God's timing, you will be in a position you're not supposed to be. You will also start comparing your life to other's lives, which will produce discontentment, fear, and jealousy.

The world can make it hard for us to keep our minds focused on Christ and away from the "need" to find someone. But don't let the pressures of anyone or anything in your life lead you outside of the timing God has for you. If someone is pressuring you to do something that you don't have peace about, you are weighing their opinion of you higher than what God's peace is telling you. It's funny how people with dysfunctional relationships try to give you advice. I mean, get your life together before you try to butt into mine, right? They say, "Well, I know what works and what doesn't work." Well, I think they need to take their own advice because I don't see anything working out for them.

When I liked someone once, I remember that one of my family members asked me how much money they made. Excuse me? That is not the first thing anyone should be thinking or asking when it comes to a potential man in your life. Nowhere in the Bible does it say that the man should be a financial provider. Yes, it says that he should provide, but he is to do this through being your spiritual protection and covering (Ephesians 5:25-27).

Let's imagine he does have a million dollars in the bank and that this was a big reason you wanted to marry him. What if, while you're away on your honeymoon, you both lose your jobs, your transmission breaks, and your house burns down? You'd be left with nothing that you initially built your marriage upon. I realize this is a drastic example, but is meant to show you that money and other worldly things that can be taken away in an instant should not be the foundation of your relationship.

Friendships are SO important in your walk and journey as a single woman. It is important to cultivate godly relationships now because, when you do get married and are in a covenant with someone, they will be able to help hold you accountable in your marriage.

The types of friendships you pursue can make or break you in many areas including temptation, comparison, and more. Do not be misled. Bad company corrupts good character (1 Corinthians 15:33). If you are hanging around people who want to "drop it like it's hot" and go to the club each Friday night, then that's a problem. The only "club" I will be going to is Club Monaco.

Friendships are incredibly essential to your journey of celibacy and being pure for Jesus. When you have the right people in your corner, it will become the norm to wait for the right one to come in God's timing. I remember when I felt out of place for not wanting to have sex with guys and felt pressured to "date just to date." But when I surrounded myself with godly friendships, it honestly was not normal to even talk about such things. I became content in Christ. I was not focused on putting a ring on it, but on putting His purpose on it.

I have been around friends who have been bitter and jealous of God's favor in my life. They didn't have their own personal relationships with God, so they didn't understand. And do you know what that did? It made me shrink down to who they were because I didn't want them to feel uncomfortable. At times, the Lord would tell me to stop talking to someone, but I would just ignore the promptings. But now that I've seen the repercussions of not listening and the spiritual fruit that came when I eventually did listen, I understand why I felt those promptings. He was trying to protect me.

Godly friends will push you in your relationship with God and will hold you accountable to your purpose. For example, when I was writing this book, my friends were an integral part of the process. They encouraged me, checked on me, and made sure that I was following the guidelines and deadline that the Lord gave me conviction for. Friends are supposed to push you closer to obedience and to what the Lord is telling you to do, not away from it.

If you have friends who aren't walking with Jesus as closely as you are, you shouldn't alter your standards because of them. For instance, when I was the maid of honor in a bridal party, it was expected for me to go to the bachelorette party. I have nothing against those, but I knew there were going to be some activities at this particular one that I wasn't morally comfortable with. Everyone knew this because I put my foot down at the beginning. You don't have to lower your values or standards for anybody but God, and He wouldn't ask you to.

So, who are your friends? Do their actions and lifestyles reflect the kind of person you want to be? You might not realize it in the moment, but you will begin to pick up and mirror their mannerisms, thought patterns, decisions, and actions. When I started hanging out with a new group of friends during my childhood, my dad picked it up right away as my character began to change.

I also remember this happening when I lived in New York City. I was hanging around a certain individual who cared a lot about the rich and famous lifestyle. The car you drove, the way you looked, and the part of town you lived in were all very important to them. As I was spending time with this person, other people close to me were telling me that I was changing, that I was becoming materialistic. I didn't see or agree with that, so I brushed it off. But that's the thing. When you are around these individuals, you might not notice the changes, but other people in your life will.

Let's say you go to a cookout and stand by the grill for a majority of the evening. When you leave, the person you see next might ask you if you were around food because they can smell the charcoal. It got into your hair and your clothes. This is an external example, but the same applies to internal changes. You pick up and absorb the things that you are around.

What are the friends around you pushing you to achieve? What are your standards for friendship? Can anyone just be your friend? In John 15:14, Jesus said, *"You are my friends if you do what I command."* This means obeying the Father. His friend factor was based on listening to and obeying God's commands.

This is extremely important. Some people might say they've surrendered their life to Him, but you'll be able to tell the truth of this by their actions. Do they follow God daily or only on Sunday mornings? We shouldn't be following God only when we feel like it, so we shouldn't surround ourselves with people who do so. If you are joined as friends with someone that is not truly following Him, then what direction are you going in? You run the risk of being badly influenced and pushed in the wrong directions.

When you share things that the Lord has placed in your heart to do, do your friends look at you like you're crazy or do they encourage you? I once shared with a friend what God had laid on my heart, and they looked at me cross eyed. They thought I was crazy. I left that conversation doubtful, wondering if I was.

A true friend will sharpen you and hold you accountable. As scriptures states in Proverbs 27:17 NIV, *"As iron sharpens iron, so one person sharpens another."*

Another important reason to have friends that are in line with God is that they will have convictions in their hearts to stay the course. When you are confronted with choices and need to make a decision about whether or not to enter certain environments or do certain things, someone with no conviction at all may persuade you to step out of the will God has for you. This can be a stumbling block, and it can also open the door for many other temptations. You might not want to do certain things, but you could end up choosing to in order to please your friends. Although we can't blame our actions on other people, it's important to surround ourselves with those who won't tempt us to stray in the first place.

You should also watch out for those who are jealous and those who covet. We shouldn't be around those people, and we should not be that person. This will limit you and your future. Friends like this will hold you back. You may shrink what you are to make the other person feel comfortable and help them hide their own insecurities. If you aren't careful, this can lead to you not being your true self. You can only practice for so long before it will become your reality.

Being around friends that have their hearts and minds set on God has helped me tremendously in my walk with Christ as a single woman. Watching how they live their lives in the purpose and calling God has for them makes it feel "normal" to be doing the things of God. This has been huge for me. When I had examples to the contrary, it made me feel alone and weird.

Having godly friendships has given me hope and peace. It can for you as well. Your contentment in Him will be strong. If you haven't grown up with godly friends, don't think it's too late for you, no matter your age. I didn't have my first set of godly friendships until I was 23. This group of friends held me accountable and pushed me closer to Jesus.

You might not currently have a swarm of friends living for God, but as you seek and pursue Him, He will align your path to ones that *"will stick closer than brother"* (Proverbs 18:24). Some of my friends are even closer to me than some of my family members. As sisters in Christ, we are part of His family.

Again, we are in this world but not of this world. We are not perfect by any means, so it is important not to look down on others. Some people might not know what they are doing is wrong. We must meet them where they are and love them. We cannot push Christ on anyone. If you have been praying for a family member or a friend to know Jesus, continue to. Do not grow weary in doing it. Only God has the power to change someone. Continue to have faith that His will be done in their lives in His timing, and continue to be the example to them that Christ would want you to be.

Chapter 8

Temptation And Sin In Your Single Season

This might be an uncomfortable topic for some of us to talk about, but it's a very important one. There are many areas of temptation and sin that we can fall into during our single seasons, but sexual sin is one of the biggest. There are so many pressures from society to go against what God commands of us in this area, but the following scriptures share God's will for us:

"For this is the will of God, your sanctification: that you abstain from sexual immorality; that each one of you know how to control his own body in holiness and honor, not in the passion of lust like the Gentiles who do not know God."
– 1 Thessalonians 4:3-5 ESV

"And so dear brothers and sisters, I plead with you to give your bodies to God because of all He has done for you. Let them be a living and holy sacrifice – the kind he will find acceptable. This is truly the way to worship him." – Romans 12:1

God commands us to wait until marriage to engage in a sexual relationship. Marriage, and therefore sexual intimacy, is meant to be a picture of how Christ loved the church (Ephesians 5:25-27). It's supposed to be faithful and sacrificial, as Christ Himself is faithful and sacrificial.

It's dangerous to submit to your flesh and go against God through sexual sin. Sex is more than just sex. When you sleep with someone, it's more than physical. It's spiritual. Your two

127

souls are connecting as one. Committing sin with our bodies through sex creates soul ties that can carry over as baggage into the relationship God calls us to.

1 Corinthians 6:16-18 NIV states, *"Do you not know that he who unites himself with a prostitute is one with her in body? For it is said, 'The two will become one flesh.' But whoever is united with the Lord is one with him in spirit. Flee from sexual immorality. All other sins a person commits are outside the body, but whoever sins sexually, sins against their own body."*

This unhealthy soul tie can come from booty calls, relationships, one-night stands, or any sex before marriage. We need to be very careful because sexual sin can cause us to feel powerless, become sadly addicted, and live in bondage.

Through intercourse in marriage, *"the two shall become one flesh"* (v.16). This is backed up by science. According to *Psychology Today*, Oxytocin, a powerful hormone triggered through physical intimacy, causes sexual partners to bond to each other. When we hug and kiss a loved one, our oxytocin levels raise. Oxytocin is also released during breastfeeding to aid in the bonding of the mother and child. If a husband and wife bond with each other sexually, their bond should increase over time. If you walk into marriage already bonded to another, you definitely won't be doing your marriage any favors.

Song of Solomon 8:4 urges us *"not to awaken love until the right time."* Why? Because the Lord wants to protect us from the consequences that come with sex outside of the committed, loving, marriage relationship mentioned above.

If you've already had sex outside of marriage, it's not too late for you. You can be a born-again virgin. I'm not a virgin. I wish I was, but I didn't have a Christ-centered view on sex until later on in life. I never talked about it with anyone, and I just did it because everyone else was and because it was the popular thing to do. But I never had a true desire for it or a peace about it.

Yes, you can use a condom or another form of birth control, but that doesn't keep you away from soul ties that will affect your life. It doesn't matter if you haven't had that example or if no one else around you is living a life of sexual purity. You can be that example. I am telling you from experience that it's not worth it to sleep with someone that is not your husband.

If you have those desires and want to act on them, remember that it is your decision not to act on them that will set you apart. It's also important to remember that not only should we abstain from sexual relations before marriage, but that we also should make a point not to dwell on or think lustful thoughts. To even think on those thoughts means you have committed the act in your heart (Matthew 5:28). That is why it's imperative for us to constantly renew our minds.

How Is It Possible to Abstain from Sex?

So now that we know God has called us to wait for marriage to have sex, the next question is, "How?" Below, I have listed several tips that will help you rule over your sex drive instead of letting it rule over you.

1. We can have fulfilling lives without sexual intimacy. For example, Jesus faced the same temptations we faced and empathizes with our weaknesses (Hebrews 4:15). Both Jesus and Paul were abstinent and had lives that were exemplary of who and what we should be as Christians. Their names are written in history. Their lives set the mark for who we are today. We are encouraged by their ministries on the streets not what they were doing in the sheets.

2. Meditate on the fact that Paul describes singleness as a desirable state (1 Corinthians 7:32-35). Are there things that you can do as a single that you wouldn't be able to do as easily if you were married? Personally, I love the freedom and intimate time I get to spend with Jesus as a single. We go as we please, and I can spend hours on end just being alone with Him through prayer, worship, mission trips, church gatherings, and more.

3. Find someone to be your mentor and/or surround yourself with community. There is safety in having accountability partners (Proverbs 11:14). This is extremely important. It is also vital that you choose these people carefully. How is their contentment in Christ, and are they bearing fruit to prove it? Again, we are not perfect, so having a mentor will help sharpen and develop us spiritually. At times, we can't see things that people close to us can. Our mentors or accountability partners can have those "hard" conversations with us that will help to steer us in the right direction.

4. Differentiate between sinful lust and the godly desire for intimacy with a husband. When you are interested in a single man, are you just thinking about how attractive he is, or are you more interested in getting to know him as a human being you may want to be with "in sickness and in health?" The latter is a godly desire. If this is a struggle for you, you have to train yourself in how you think about men.

5. Remember that marriage and sex don't solve our problems. Television shows and movies seem to be preoccupied with telling us that all we need is to "find someone" and all our emotional issues will go away. Consider going on a media fast or being more selective about the media you consume. Think about the reality shows, books, movies, or music that you indulge in. Ask yourself, "What is this

telling me about sex and relationships?" If they don't line up with God's view, it might be best to stay away from those things.

6. Ask God to help you through it. If you're praying for God to take away your sex drive, revise your prayers. Sexuality is a biological function. Praying for God to remove your sex drive is sort of like praying that your hair will never turn gray. Rather than praying for that, pray to overcome some of the struggles that may be leading you to have overwhelming sexual urges. Is loneliness a contributing factor? Is it anger or bitterness?

It is my hope and prayer that these suggestions will help you control your sexual desires and align yourself to God when it comes to this area of life.

Breaking Free from Soul Ties

As previously mentioned, a soul tie is when two souls are being knitted together and becoming one flesh. It's a connection that binds two individuals together, saved or unsaved.

"You say, 'Food for the stomach and the stomach for food, and God will destroy them both.' The body, however, is not meant for sexual immorality but for the Lord, and the Lord for the body. By his power God raised the Lord from the dead, and he will raise us also. Do you not know that your bodies are members of Christ himself? Shall I then take the members of Christ and unite them with a prostitute? Never! Do you not know that he who unites himself with a prostitute is one with her in body? For it is said, 'The two will become one flesh.' But whoever is united with the Lord is one with him in spirit."

Flee from sexual immorality. All other sins a person commits are outside the body, but whoever sins sexually, sins against their own body. Do you not know that your bodies are temples of the Holy Spirit, who is in you, whom you have received from God? You are not your own; you *were bought at a price. Therefore, honor God with your bodies."* - 1 Corinthians 6:13 – 20 NIV

Our bodies are not our own. They are made to bring God glory. Maybe you're thinking, "You see, this is my body and I can do whatever I want to do with MY body." Remember, we just read right here that our body is not ours. Or maybe you're thoughts are something like, "But I can have sex with whoever I want to." Remember, we just read that our body is connected to God and that members of Christ shouldn't be connected to a prostitute. Even if you think you're "making love," it's not true love outside of marriage. It's more than just "having sex." It's more serious than you think. It's deeply spiritual.

Married couples come together as one – *"and the two should become one flesh"* (Mark 10:8 ESV). This bond shouldn't be broken by man. According to Mark 10:9, what God puts together no man should tear apart. Marriage is ordained by God. If God has put two together and no man is supposed to bring them apart, then two unmarried people that join together are outside of the covenant and protection that God has intended.

If you are currently entangled with someone that you have no business associating with, it's time you break this soul tie now. You don't even have to have sex with someone to have a soul tie. Just sharing intimate conversations with someone and spending time with them can produce an emotional soul tie. Sharing things creates a bond. According to

Luke 6:45, out of the abundance of your heart, your mouth speaks. The more you share, the more you will be connected. When you share that bond, you are creating that intimacy.

"As soon as he had finished speaking to Saul, the soul of Jonathon was knit to the soul of David, and Jonathan loved him as his own soul." - 1 Samuel 18:1 ESV

Soul ties can also apply to platonic friendships, just like in the case of Jonathan and David. If you are connected to something and unable to break that connection, then you are tied to it. That is why it's difficult for you to break it. It's time to get serious about breaking these unhealthy soul ties.

What's the cure?

1. Acknowledge that you have a problem.

Galatians 3:13 says, *"Christ has redeemed us from the curse pronounced by the law. When he was hung on the cross, He took upon himself the curse for our wrongdoing."*

Believers are not to be cursed. If you are one with Christ, then you stand with Him in righteousness.

If you find yourself in an unhealthy soul tie, you don't have to stay in it. You have the authority in Christ to say that you won't give in to it. This first involves recognizing and acknowledging both the existence and the problem of the soul tie.

2. Repent of your sins.

Confess any and all ungodly soul ties to the Lord. 1 John 1:9 says: *"If we confess our sins, he is faithful and just and will forgive us our sins and purify us from all unrighteousness."*

This verse tells us that the only condition to God's forgiveness is that we repent. He is faithful and righteous to forgive, which means He removes the debt of our sins and cleanses us from it.

"If anyone is in Christ, he is a new creation. The old has passed away; behold, the new has come."
– 2 Corinthians 5:17 ESV

When someone tries to remind you of your past, tell them that it is just that - your past. Recognize and find confidence in the fact that you are living a new life.

3. Stop feeding the connection.

Make a solemn and sincere commitment to the Lord to break off any relationship that is not pure or righteous in His eyes. Follow through on that commitment. Denounce all relationships that are not good.

Whatever you feed will grow. Throw away your sexually explicit CDs or anything else that is tempting you to fall back. Stop going out with or texting the person that is tempting you into sexual sin. If you give the enemy even a small open door, lust can run rampant. You're going to need strong boundaries and discipline.

4. Renew your mind and practice living a life of consecration.

This means there are some things you shouldn't do and some places that you shouldn't go. Romans 12:1 says: *"Therefore, I urge you, brothers and sisters, in view of God's mercy, to offer your bodies as a living sacrifice, holy and pleasing to God – this is your true and proper worship*

This is our honorable service. You can't expect to stay free from a soul tie if you don't understand the deeply rooted purpose of why the body was created.

5. Seek God's deliverance

It's the will of the Lord for us to be set free. You can be set free if you choose to. What do you plan on passing down to your children? You may think that it only affects you, but your decisions will have an impact on generations to come (Numbers 14:18). What are you practicing right now that your children could one day emulate? Do you want your children to go through what you have gone through? Even if you were raised in a broken home, your home doesn't have to look like what you grew up in. This is not meant to bash parents who have a past, but it is meant to hold us all accountable to what we now know. Your soul does not have to be tied to someone. Pray for all ungodly soul ties to be released. It can be broken through the power and authority of Jesus Christ.

No Sin in the City

So, what exactly is sin? Sin is rebellion against God. It's doing the exact opposite of His commands. Scripture doesn't define sin by giving us a long list of do's and don'ts. Instead, it shows us the way Jesus lives and how He calls us to live. The spiritual principles by which He lives are the same standards of conduct that He expects His human creations to live by.

The most basic definition of sin can be found in 1 John 3:4: *"Everyone who sins is breaking God's law, for all sin is contrary to the law of God."*

In this verse, God defines a boundary for all mankind. He says that sin is going against His holy, spiritual law (Romans 7:12-14). Crossing that boundary God set for us is sin. He didn't do it to punish us or to be evil. He set those limits for our protection. He did it to show His love for us. Those laws define how we demonstrate love to God and to our neighbors (Deuteronomy 30:15-16, Matthew 22:35-40, 1 John 5:3). Sin is a violation of that law of love. God showed us a way to live in peace and harmony with Him and with mankind. He defined this way of life by His law. When we sin, we violate that boundary and break God's law.

We should realize that sin starts in the mind. When we allow evil thoughts to enter our minds and stay there, these evil thoughts can eventually spring into action, leading us to sin.

The Word says that we are what we think (Proverbs 23:7). Sin pollutes our minds and hearts and causes them to not be pure before God. Sin distracts us and keeps our minds on the relationships we don't have, rather than our relationship with Christ.

You might think that you sin by the things you do, but you can also sin by the things you don't do. James 4:17 says, *"It is a sin to know what you ought to do and then not do it."* In this verse, James is telling us that if we recognize that we should to be doing certain things but don't, the failure to do them is a sin. We are not meeting the standard God has set for us.

The Greek word for sin is "hamartia." According to Merriam-Webster Dictionary, the word origin and history for hamartia means "to miss the mark." In archery, the word sin is commonly used when someone has missed the mark. When an archer shoots a bow and it lands off target, they would call out "sin," meaning they missed the mark. When we sin, we are missing the mark by falling short of God's commandments.

However, no one is perfect. When we do miss the mark, as believers, we are in the boundaries of God's grace. We should be continuously striving for our actions to be in line with God and not intentionally abusing the grace given to us.

The process of training yourself to stay away from sin is not easy, and there will be a fight. But our battle isn't against flesh and blood. It is a spiritual fight (Ephesians 6:12). Everything in the spiritual dictates the natural. Just as scripture states, *"Truly I tell you, whatever you bind on earth will be bound in heaven,*

and whatever you lose on earth will be loosed in heaven." –
Matthew 18:18 NIV

"If you do what is right, will you not be accepted? But if you do
not do what is right, sin is crouching at your door; it desires to
have you, but you must rule over it."
– Genesis 4:7 NIV

As the verse states, *"sin is crouching at your door."* You don't have to find sin because sin has already found you. For example, I've watched over toddlers who have said that their parents told them they could have candy. I knew this was untrue because their parents told me specifically that they could not have any at that time. The child just wanted the candy in the moment, so they said what they could to get it. They weren't trying to do any harm, but it just naturally came out.

Sometimes we feel like we are born a "certain way," desiring things contrary to God's Word. It feels natural to us, so we take it on as our identity. "Maybe this is the way I am. There is nothing I can do about it." The first part of this is true because we are born into sin, but that is why it's important to be "born again" in Him, who makes us all a new creation (2 Corinthians 5:17).

The enemy is not afraid of who you are, but he is afraid of who you are becoming. He already knows the plans that God has for you. It will be easier to be deceived if you are not aware of this. As stated in the previous verse, Genesis 4:7, if you don't master sin, it will master you.

I have a York Shirer Terrier named Frankie. When I tell him to sit, he sits. He knows who his master is. If you understand that your authority comes from God, you can do the same thing. It comes down to what you believe. Resist the devil, and He will flee from you (James 4:7).

The Bible also states, *"Be on the alert. Stand firm in the faith... be strong."* – 1 Corinthians 16:13 NASB

To *"be on the alert"* in this context, means to know what tempts you so that you can stay away from it. It is so important to develop strength in this area because the enemy is always on the prowl. In fact, his intentions are only to *"kill, steal, and destroy"* (John 10:10). God gives us a defense in this. He gives us armor that will protect us. Again, temptations and tests will come, but God always gives us a way out. We are equipped with the armor He has given us. It's our choice to put it on.

> *"Finally, be strong in the Lord and His almighty power. Put on the full armor of God, so that you can take your stand against the enemy's schemes. For our struggle isn't against flesh and blood, but against the rulers, against the powers of this dark world and against the spiritual forces of evil in the heavenly realms. Therefore, put on the full armor of God, so that when the day of evil comes, you may be able to stand your ground, and after you have done everything, to stand. Stand firm then, with the belt of truth buckled around*

your waist, with the breastplate of righteousness in place, and with your feet fitted with the readiness that comes from the gospel of peace. In addition to all of this, take up the shield of faith, with which you can extinguish all the flaming arrows of the evil one. Take the helmet of salvation and the sword of the Spirit, which is the word of God." – Ephesians 6:10-18

The Meaning of Righteousness

Matthew 6:33 says, *"Seek the Kingdom of God above all else and live righteously, and he will give you everything you need."* Maybe you often hear this verse and understand what it means to seek the kingdom but are not familiar of the meaning of righteousness. So, what is righteousness?

The Merriam Webster Dictionary defines righteousness as, "Behavior that is morally justifiable or right." The Bible's standard of human righteousness is God's own perfection carried out in every attribute, every attitude, every behavior, and every word. Thus, God's laws describe His own character and what He measures as human righteousness. We are never perfect, but through the blood of Christ we can become righteous.

"God made him who had no sin to be sin for us, so that in him we might become the righteousness of God."
– 2 Corinthians 5:21 NIV

This is an amazing truth. On the cross, Jesus exchanged our sin for His perfect righteousness. One day when we stand before God, He will see not our sin, but He will see the holy righteousness of Jesus.

You are either in right standing or you are not. Righteousness becomes the product of our holiness. When you walk in right standing, in righteousness, it positions you in holiness. When you pursue holiness, God knows He can trust you. When your heart is right, you can't go wrong. A heart surrendered to Him is a heart He can trust. The Lord can't trust you with a person if He can't trust you with yourself. You have to surrender to the process.

The Lord Is Open for Delivery

The Lord is our deliverer from any troubles, addictions, or strongholds we may have. God can deliver you from whatever is holding you down, if you let Him. Sometimes we like our sin and want to stay in it, but we can release it to Him if we want to.

"Then they cried out to the LORD in their trouble, and he delivered them from their distress."
- Psalm 107:6 NIV

David sang to the Lord the words of this song when the Lord delivered him from the hand of all his enemies and from the hand of Saul. He said:

"The Lord is my rock, my fortress and my deliverer;
my God is my rock, in whom I take refuge,
my shield and the horn of my salvation.
He is my stronghold, my refuge and my savior—
from violent people you save me."
- 2 Samuel 22:2-3 NIV

As you are discovering more of who you are in Christ, you might see some dark areas of your life that need to be exposed. This is an important part of spending time with God and developing in your relationship with Him.

Maybe there are some things in your past holding you back that you need to be set free from. I don't know what this looks like for you, whether it's hanging out with friends at the club, a pornography addiction, an anger problem, or something else entirely. Maybe you just saw your ex-boyfriend and thought, "Man, I was about to take off all my clothes just by looking at him." Within all of these things, the enemy might try to tell you that you haven't been saved "for real" because you were having those thoughts. Know that temptation will always be there. Just because you are tempted by something doesn't mean that you are not delivered from it. It's your actions of not pursuing or fulfilling that temptation that show if you are really free. That is why the Word says to flee from temptation (James 4:7).

Here are some scriptures to focus and meditate on if you are struggling with temptation:

"Run from anything that stimulates youthful lusts. Instead, pursue righteous living, faithfulness, love, and peace. Enjoy the companionship of those who call on the Lord with pure hearts. Again I say, don't get involved in foolish, ignorant arguments that only start fights. A servant of the Lord must not quarrel but must be kind to everyone, be able to teach, and be patient with difficult people." - Timothy 2:22-24

"Watch and pray so that you will not fall into temptation. The spirit is willing, but the flesh is weak."
– Matthew 26:41 NIV

"But I say, walk by the spirit, and you will not gratify the desires of the flesh." - Galatians 5:16 ESV

"No temptation has overtaken you except what is common to man. And God is faithful; he will not let you be tempted beyond what you can bear. But when you are tempted, he will also provide a way out so that you can endure it." -1
Corinthians 10:13 NIV

When you do see progression in the areas that you are challenged in, know that it was by God's GRACE that you didn't succumb to that temptation. It was by God's GRACE that you didn't open up your mouth and curse out someone that offended you. It was by God's GRACE that instead of stealing those paper clips at work, you went and bought your own at Staples. You see, when you are delivered, you will by God's grace do all these things.

We will all be tempted, but God gives us a way out. Are you taking advantage of the ways out? As you are moving along in your journey, take advantage of the opportunities God gives you to flee the temptations, whether it's through a new community of godly friends, a Bible-based church, or whatever He brings to you in that moment. You don't want to bring your baggage into the next season.

Chapter 9:

Guarding Your Heart

Through all that we have learned so far, it's important that we take guard and protect our hearts. We can have all the knowledge in the world and memorize every scripture, but knowledge alone is not power. Applied knowledge is power. In order for us to consistently apply what we learn, we must guard our hearts.

"Guard your heart above all else, for it determines the course of your life." – Proverbs 4:23

This scripture doesn't say for your mom, your teacher, your grandparents, or your best friend to guard your heart. It says that *you* should guard your heart. We each are responsible for our own hearts, and we must take the action of guarding it. As the scripture says, the state of your heart determines the path the rest of your life will take. That's huge. That's significant. Society tells us that choosing a certain career, whether it's being a doctor or a CEO, will set you up for life because you will be financially covered. But we have to dig deeper than that. It is the state of our hearts that truly determines what the fruit of our lives will be.

How do we guard our hearts? There are five key ways you can do this: surround yourself with like-minded people, fill your mind with Christ-like forms of entertainment, avoid comparing your life to the lives of others, stand guard to social media, and immerse yourself in scripture.

Surround Yourself with Like-Minded People

As we discussed previously, it is imperative to surround yourself with like-minded people. This plays a large part in guarding our hearts.

Maybe your parents are trying to tell you to do things that you know don't align with the Word of God. Maybe you have a pattern of divorce in your family that traces all the way back to your great grandparents. You can see that following their examples and advice will lead to bad fruit. Maybe they are pushing you to do things that are not morally right in order to excel in your career or gain a better social life. Maybe they are pressuring you by using the verse, *"Honor your father and mother"* (Ephesians 6:1). Know that this verse would only be applicable if they are coming from a foundation built on Christ and if they reflect that through their actions and decisions.

Another area of this is your friendships. You pick up the habits of those you hang around the most, as we mentioned in an earlier chapter. Essentially, you turn into the people you are around. If you place yourself in a toxic environment, you are not guarding your heart. For example, listening to music that doesn't glorify God or being around men when you know it will lead you to temptation could both represent toxic environments.

When I was in New York, even though I had some bad influences, I met amazing friends that drew me closer to Christ toward the end of my season there. They were my first examples of godly friendships. Little did I know, God used that period to help me develop in Him and prepare me for the next season. Eventually, I realized that I could really live for Christ and guard my heart without feeling alone. Being around like-minded people can sharpen you and push you to develop spiritually. You can also relate to one another by sharing your struggles and triumphs.

Surrounding yourself with people whose eyes are set on Christ is an important part of guarding your heart. Choose to protect your heart with the company you keep.

Fill Your Mind with Christ-Like Forms of Entertainment

Remaining pure of heart starts in our minds. It is imperative to protect ourselves from secular forms of entertainment that might influence us to sin.

Do you find yourself having lustful thoughts? Do you feel depressed after a break up? Is the kind of music that you choose to listen to helpful? Lyrics like, "Do you wanna rub me down?" are so common in mainstream media these days and can be extremely toxic to you.

Do you feel like it's okay to do certain things that are contrary to the word of God because "everyone is doing it"? Pay attention to what television shows and movies you are watching. I have to be so careful to not even watch things with sexually explicit content because my heart and mind are so sensitive to it. I have to close my eyes or walk away. I literally cringe at that kind of content.

You may feel like there isn't any Christian music out there that you like. I feel you, 100 percent. I used to think the same thing. For example, I like to listen to upbeat, powerful music when working out. I thought that would be hard to find in this genre, but I was wrong!

When I first started to transfer over from secular to Christian music, I began with Christian rap, then I listened to gospel, and then I worked my way to contemporary. I had to ease into it. It was a process.

I didn't know many artists at first because I hadn't previously been exposed to this genre of music. I only knew what we sang in church, but that felt too adult for me. I wanted younger, more "hip" music. Soon, I was introduced to Hillsong, Bethel, Jesus Culture, Kari Jobe, Stephanie Frizzell, and more. If you are looking for somewhere to get started, any of these would be great options. I definitely recommend checking out their music and albums. It just might change your life.

Soon, I began to crave that music. I found it so uplifting. I didn't just listen to it in the privacy of my own home. I had it on when I went out and about. I wasn't embarrassed playing it in public because I was able to vibe with it. I also started to go to Christian concerts when my favorite artists were in town. I'll go ahead and warn you, you might soon be stalking dates of tours to find out when they will be in your city.

If you think that going to these concerts won't influence you and have an impact on your life, think again. It's a worship experience. There are spirits floating around in that atmosphere. You are singing words to songs like you are at a church. Subconsciously, you are letting that positive energy come into your atmosphere. There is so much more to music than you might realize.

If the radio is your weakness, I recommended purchasing CDs to play in your car. This will uplift you. You could also download a Christian podcast and listen to that. Think about anything that will encourage you and help you set your mind on Him, and make that what you choose to listen to. When it comes to Christian forms of media and entertainment, anything that brings you closer to Him is a winner.

Avoid Comparing Your Life to the Lives of Others

When we start comparing, we are trying to please others. When we try to please others, we are living our lives for them instead of for God. We start to believe that we are missing out on something. Have you thought like that before? I have. Can I be transparent with you?

I have had moments of weakness where I thought I was being dealt the short end of the stick. There was a time in my life when men made no advances toward me at all – like, none. It was okay at first, but then I'd see other women getting stuff, such as designers handbags and paid rent, and I'd be like, "Hey now, can I get a dolla?" I couldn't understand it. But soon, I realized that sleeping with men came with a price. You devalue your worth when you prostitute yourself either socially or sexually in exchange for anything. When I learned that lesson, I was thankful I didn't get wrapped up in all that. God was protecting me. He had a veil over me so no one could talk to me. Guys see me, but they just don't see me like that. The right one will, in God's timing.

Growing up, I went to a Christian middle school where so many of my peers were more articulate with their thoughts and prayed better than I could. Their lives with Christ seemed so mature. I knew we were the same age, but they seemed further along than me. This crippled me and made me stop growing. Now I understand that we all grow at different rates. I shouldn't have let that discourage me. There will always be someone smarter, wiser, or more articulate. But we need to stay and be confident in our lane while still congratulating others and celebrating their growth and success.

In another instance, I applied for a flight attendant position with a private airline right after college. When I went in for the interview, I also went with two people I knew. I definitely thought that should have been offered the job above them because I felt more qualified. However, they both received a position and I never received a call back. I was so upset when I didn't get it, and I just couldn't understand why. It had already been a difficult season, and that was the last straw for me. I didn't realize it in the moment, but God had different plans for me. He had something better for me. It was actually good that I didn't get that position because it would have been wasted time.

So, what was I missing out on in both of these circumstances? I was missing out on having peace and on resting in Him. What are you missing out on? Comparison will steal your contentment very quickly. It will divert your focus to the next season before you're ready for it and before God's timing. Focus on your portion and on being faithful with what you have and where you're at now.

The above examples show instances where I was tempted to feel less than others. However, there's another kind of comparison we should watch out for — being overly confident and thinking we're superior to others.

Maybe you've received an award or some kind of recognition that caused you to think that you are "all that." God has a way of humbling you quickly in these kinds of situations. Don't ever think you have arrived. Pride comes before the fall (Proverbs 16:18). Being overly confident can cause you to become prideful.

*"Make a careful exploration of who you are and the work you have been given, and then sink yourself into that. **Don't be impressed with yourself. Don't compare yourself with others.** Each of you must take responsibility for doing the creative best you can with your own life."* – Galatians 6:4-5

As you can see, you must not compare yourself with others. We must never be impressed with ourselves. We must not become prideful. This is extremely crucial. Satan was kicked out of heaven because of pride (Ezekiel 28:17-19). He was prideful because he felt that God shouldn't be receiving all the glory and praise. He wanted the glory for himself. This stemmed out of jealousy. He used the gifts God gave him to bring glory to himself. We must always know that it's God's work in us that makes us who we are, not our own efforts.

Stand Guard to Social Media

Maybe you need to fast from social media if it's causing you to become distracted and discontent. Fasting is abstaining from something and using that time to pray and pursue God instead. Jesus fasted for forty days in the wilderness to receive direction from the Lord. He did this to rid himself of any distractions and make sure that He was hearing from God accurately. His fast was from food and water. You can fast from things that God is leading you to fast from. Just because someone else is fasting from a certain thing doesn't mean you have to follow the same route. Do what God is leading you to do.

Fasting from social media can involve deleting the app from your phone, setting time limits for when you go on, or entirely staying away from it for a while.

Think about the ways you use social media. Why are you posting what you post? Is it to get the likes and approval of others? In an affirmation-saturated world, our social media lives can quickly become about how many followers we have, who liked our statuses, and the amount of interaction and comments we get on our pages. There are now even opportunities to buy followers instead of growing them organically. Why would you pay for this? So you can seem important?

It can be so easy for us to become attached to social media that the first thing we do in the morning is check our newsfeeds instead of reading the Bible. Are you more dependent on social media for your spiritual fix than you are on God and time spent with Him? Twitter should not be where we turn for guidance and answers to our prayers.

Even if you're using social media for healthy reasons, it can still have a hold on you if you are glued to it more than you are glued to and present in real life. For example, maybe you invited someone over but kept your eyes glued to your phone instead of giving them your undivided attention. Have you ever been to a function where everyone was on their phones? This can hinder us from living in the moment.

Social media can also lead to comparison and envy. Are you friends with your ex on Facebook? Do you find yourself checking up on them more often than you should? You don't have to look at their page every five seconds to see how they are doing. More likely than not, they are fine. You have to guard and protect your heart in this area. I have seen too many people that I know go through this when they didn't have to.

For all of these reasons, carefully monitoring the ways we view and use social media is key in guarding our hearts.

Immerse Yourself in Scripture

A beautiful vision of what life can look like as we immerse our self in scripture is found in Psalm 1:2-3 NIV:

"...but whose delight is in the law of the Lord, and who meditates on his law day and night. That person is like a tree planted by streams of water, which yields its fruit in season and whose leaf does not wither - whatever they do prospers."

Scripture will never become irrelevant or out of date. It is far more than just words on a page. If we believe in scripture and apply it to our lives, it is truly powerful. We must trust in and follow what it says. Even demons believe and know scripture, but they do not revere God (James 2:19). He doesn't live in their hearts. Demons cringe at the sound of scripture. It's the most POWERFUL weapon we have. It will never lose its potency.

One way that you can meditate on scripture is by writing verses on notecards and leaving them around your house. You can even memorize those scriptures for the spiritual attacks that come your way. You don't have to wait until you are attacked or in bad a situation to become familiar with the Word. You can have scripture ingrained in your mind so that you know what the Word says when trials do come.

Knowing scripture will also keep you from being deceived. You will be able to discern when anyone comes to you quoting or using scripture out of context. I encourage you to look up and read every verse I have used in this book and make sure that it is in alignment with Christ. When you are in church, do the same.

Where does scripture come from? The Bible. If you don't have one already, get a Bible you can read and understand. Immersing yourself in scripture is the most significant part of guarding your heart.

We have to guard our hearts - just as we would guard our homes from burglars, just as there are guards that protect the queen of England, just as we put a case around our phones to guard them if they drop. The enemy is roaring around like a lion, looking to destroy. He knows your weak spots. He wants to make you doubtful, fearful, and confused. If you aren't guarding your heart, he can get in. We don't want to leave him any open doors. Guarding your heart is key in being content and confident in Christ.

*"Then you will experience God's peace, which exceeds anything we can understand. His peace will **guard your hearts** and minds as you live in Christ Jesus."* – Philippians 4:7

Chapter 10

Live A Life Worthy Of Your Calling

Remaining content in the season God has you and finding your true calling, value, and purpose in Him involves a daily renewing of your mind. God doesn't renew your mind — you have to do it. You do this by meditating on the things of the Lord and by seeking daily direction from Him. He is where your true joy can be found, even in the midst of hardships, trials, and chaos.

We must guard our hearts, renew our minds, and keep a close knit of friends and mentors that push us toward Christ and remind us to be intentional in our faith walk. This is done through setting boundaries, consistently spending time with God, and being accountable to individuals we trust. Remember that that in all things we do, we do them to bring glory to God.

It's a journey. Don't give up. Don't settle. Don't fall back. Even if you do, you can always come back on the path. I am rooting for you. Stay the course, and do not grow weary in doing good. God loves you no matter what, and He is here for you.

As you finish reading this book, I want to encourage you to think about the topics we covered and be honest with yourself about which ones you can improve upon. None of us are perfect. I am not perfect. Having an awareness of our areas of weakness can help us in knowing how to move forward. I also want to encourage you to highlight parts that stood out to you and share those with someone else. What did you learn? What challenged you? What inspired you? Don't just put this book back on the shelf and never think about it again. Reach out to a friend and encourage them. They will be so grateful. Just that act in itself will bring glory to Christ.

"I therefore, a prisoner for the Lord, urge you to walk in a manner worthy of the calling to which you have been called."
– Ephesians 4:1 ESV

I would like to end this book with scripture that you can pray over yourself. I want you to lead a life worthy of your calling and walk in a manner worthy of the calling that you have received. Everyone's journey with God is different. There is no formula or blue print for it all. However, I know that as you stay close to Him and obey Him in each step, you will grow in your faith and contentment in Him. I encourage you to pray these scriptures over yourself and hold them close to your heart.

"So let's not get tired of doing what is good. At just the right time we will reap a harvest of blessing if we don't give up. Therefore, whenever we have the opportunity, we should do good to everyone – especially to those in the family of faith." – Galatians 6:9-10

"So we have not stopped praying for you since we first heard about you. We ask God to give you complete knowledge of his will and to give you spiritual wisdom and

understanding. Then the way you live will always honor and please the Lord, and your lives will produce every kind of good fruit. All the while, you will grow as you learn to know God better and better. We also pray that you will be strengthened with all his glorious power so you will have all the endurance and patience you need. May you be filled with joy, and always thanking the Father. He has enabled you to share in the inheritance that belongs to his people, who live in the light. For he has rescued us from the kingdom of darkness and transferred us into the Kingdom of their dear Son, who purchased our freedom and forgave our sins." – Colossians 1:9-14

"When I think of all this, I fall to my knees and pray to the Father, the Creator of everything in heaven and on earth. I pray that from his glorious, unlimited resources he will empower you with inner strength through his Spirit. Then Christ will make his home in your hearts as you trust in him. Your roots will grow down into God's love and keep you strong. And may you have the power to understand, as all God's people should, how wide, how long, how high, and how deep his love is.

May you experience the love of Christ, though it is too great to understand fully. Then you will be made complete with all the fullness of life and power that comes from God. Now all glory to God, who is able, through his mighty power to work within us, to accomplish infinitely more than we might ask or think. Glory to him in the church and in Christ Jesus through all generations forever and ever! Amen." - Ephesians 3:14-20

"Always be full of joy in the Lord. I say it again—rejoice! Let everyone see that you are considerate in all you do. Remember, the Lord is coming soon. Don't worry about anything; instead, pray about everything. Tell God what you need, and thank him for all he has done. Then you will experience God's peace, which exceeds anything we can understand. His peace will guard your hearts and minds as you live in Christ Jesus.

And now, dear brothers and sisters, one final thing. Fix your thoughts on what is true, and honorable, and right, and pure, and lovely, and admirable. Think about things that are excellent and worthy of praise. Keep putting into practice all you learned and received from me—everything you heard from me and saw me doing. Then the God of peace will be with you." – Philippians 4:4-9

Dear Sister:

You've Got Mail

Hearing testimonies of women from around the world who are content in Christ has always been encouraging to me, especially when hearing differences in culture and background. The following are letters written by women from every continent. I pray that these letters inspire you. I pray that that they will encourage you in the season that you are in. Each of these letters were written to show you how possible it is to live in purpose while single. I hope they encourage and challenge you to be content in Christ during your singleness and to fully chase after the plans and purpose that He has for you!

Dear Sister,

There is a battle raging against your heart. The enemy will strive to choke the life out of *your* battle for contentment, but do not fear; God is your defender.

In Korea, people get married any time from right after college (in some extreme cases) to in their mid-30s (in other extreme cases). I am 33 and without a husband. I am overweight by Korean standards, which, according to my family and a culture that places a woman's worth on her appearance, means I will not be able to find "Class-A" husband material.

My grandmother, mom, and former Sunday school teacher have been praying for my future husband since I was very young. This gave me hope that I will be able to find the best man out there to be my husband. That is the first reason I do not worry. The second reason is that I trust in God. It is as simple as that. How can He not keep me, as the apple of His eye?

God actually gave me a dream while I was in South Africa with my parents on a volunteering trip. In this dream, I was able to visit an orphanage and God gave me a heart for orphans — not only to set up orphanages, but also to adopt orphans and provide a loving environment through our family! I have confidence God will bring this to pass. Because of this dream, I do not worry about whether or not God will take care of me or whether or not God will provide a husband for me.

My message to you is this: You should not be worried about marriage. Instead, enjoy life. Fix yourself up pretty every now and then — just for the pleasure of it. Enjoy social events. Take care of your body and feel good about it. Most importantly, take care of your heart and your spirit. The heart is where the issues of life come from, and the spirit is where the Word of God finds a nesting place. Let your thoughts be healthy, and form a strong enough relationship with God so that your spirit can govern your heart. In other words, keep a level head, heart, and spirit at all times.

It would be a lie to say I do not feel a bit of sadness at times. But every time I do, I am reminded of the truth that I am found in Christ. I hold on to the promise that God is in control. After everything, you are already home, because God has brought you to a place of impenetrable peace in your heart.

Always,
Sooky Park
Seoul, South Korea

Dear Sister,

Being a single woman in my 30s and a single mum, I am the happiest I have ever been. I can honestly say that I can give God all the glory. Through Him, I have an unexplainable peace, and with that also comes great joy. This was not something that happened overnight. It has been a work in progress.

I am from a mixed background. My mum is black Caribbean and my dad is white British. My parents were not married, and I would say they didn't have much of a relationship with God. My dad left my mum when I was 13 years old. Although I didn't realize it at the time, it started a desire in me to be wanted by men and to look to them to fill the void of my dad not being around.

From the age of 15 until a year ago, I had constantly been in a relationship. If I wasn't in a relationship, then I was seeing someone casually. At 27, I became a Christian and decided I wanted to do things God's way because I had made such a mess doing it on my own. Relationships have been my biggest challenge as a child of God.

My 27 years in the flesh outweighed my new relationship with God. I had always associated love with sex, and I desperately needed God to renew my understanding of real love, of His love.

Even though I wanted God's best for me, my heart had not yet been transformed. I was still doing everything in my own strength. I was still looking for men to complete me. So when a nice man came across my path, I allowed my emotions to take over. As a Christian, I entered into a relationship with a non-believer. I told myself it was okay because he had started coming to church and had gotten saved over a period of Sundays. This was great! I had a man I could have a future with, I thought. But this was not to be the case; I had built my foundation with this man on sand. It was only a matter of time before everything came crashing down. I became pregnant a month into our relationship.

It was at this point I started the biggest tribulation of my life. Before getting pregnant, I was a professional dancer and served at my church in London on the dance team. I was heavily involved and committed to serving in church. The dance team was my family. Having this baby would change everything. I wasn't mentally, emotionally, financially, or spiritually prepared for this. I condemned myself over and over again. What would everyone think of me? I distanced myself from my friends in church. As a result, my relationship with God was tested. How could I have a baby out of marriage and still be a Christian?

Once my daughter was born, life as I knew it was over. Seven months after her birth, I was left to be a single mum. I was devastated. My desire to be married and have a family was gone, and I couldn't do anything about it. Thoughts of rejection and emptiness took over. I felt unloved and unwanted, left with a baby to raise on my own. What was I going to do? The only thing I could do was cry out to God.

My first year as a mother completely changed my relationship with God. I was now separated from the dance team, as I was the only one who had a baby. Instead of sitting with everyone else in the auditorium, I was now sitting in a separate room with the other mums and babies. I couldn't even get through a sermon without it being interrupted. My worship life, which is my favorite thing as a child of God, was gone. What was the point of me even being there?

I soon realized that my relationship with God had been heavily based on my friends and my dance team. Without them around, my relationship with God was virtually nonexistent. This had to change. When it did, God was able to start His work in me. I found comfort in my situations with God. I would listen to worship music and just cry as the words of the song wrapped around my heart. Before, I never really saw God as a Father because I didn't have one. He became the Father I never had growing up. He showed me that I am loved, that He is for me, and that my current circumstances are not a reflection of who God is and how good He is.

Through my pain of being a single mother in my 30s, I went to the only person that can heal a broken heart. Through prayer and praise, God has given me his peace. It is a peace that I do not understand but that I hold on to. God restored everything the devil thought he could take from me. My identity is no longer in a man, but in Christ Jesus. I know my worth as a woman, and I am no longer scared of what the future holds. There is still the odd moment when I will end up in tears, but I always go back to God's love and His purpose for me. I know that God works all things together for His glory. Yes, I am a single mum in my 30s, and I have so much joy because I know who my Father is.

Love,

Serina

Your sister from *London, England*

Dear Sister,

In the middle of 2011, I suffered from symptoms that included temporary paralysis, slurred speech, tingling in my palms and the bottom of my feet, and temporary loss of vision. I saw a general practitioner who referred my case to a neurologist. In late 2012, he began testing for Multiple Sclerosis. At that time, I was 26 years old and had a 4-year old daughter. I was already a single mother living in Brisbane, Australia. I had no family, just a few close friends, and now this was being thrown at me. I was tested for most sexually transmitted infections after my failed long-term relationship with my daughter's father. I caught him in bed with a woman he would go on to marry. I know, right? It's hard having your long-term plan changed without you being consulted.

After more than a year of MRI tests, other neurological testing, and no diagnosis, I gave up. The only explanation was that I was suffering from conversion disorder, which is when your body exhibits physical symptoms caused by psychological pain. I had been drowning in my relationship, and when it ended in December 2011, I struggled to cope. It continued to get worse, and I didn't want to tell people about it. I was worried they would think I was feeling sorry for myself. For the most part, only my closest friends supported me through it. I felt a deep sense of loss. I had become serious about my relationship with Christ prior to the relationship ending. To be honest, our values were no longer aligned. I guess I just wanted more time to process that.

Now, looking back, I see how God was there the whole time. It was only when that season ended that I could see His unfailing love and compassion for my life. I felt that no one truly understood. I felt that people thought I deserved to be treated badly on account of me feeling so sure of myself, which came from a good dose of self-confidence I inherited from my upbringing. You see, from a young age, I always knew that I wanted to be treasured. I desired to be valued and wanted by the people in my life. My parents, and my father in particular, encouraged that. I didn't always know what that looked like, but I tended to make my exit if I decided I it wasn't present. I would later realize that, figuratively, I had brought a knife to a gun fight.

So it is no surprise that I considered suicide to end my life. I had somehow, somewhere along the lines, pinned my worth to the feelings that someone had for me. I had put us both in separate cages. Subconsciously, my brain was telling my body I couldn't live without a person that clearly did not want to be in the relationship. I had to affirm to myself that my worth was not found in a relationship. My worth was found in the One who made me. I had to remind myself that I still had so much to offer to the world and to my daughter. I knew that God still had a plan for my life and that I would find peace and love in due season. Now, four years later, I realize that Christ is in fact enough and, "What is more, I consider everything as a loss *because of the surpassing worth of knowing Christ Jesus my Lord, for whose sake I have lost all things. I consider them garbage, that I may gain Christ"* (Philippians 3:8 NIV).

Kind regards,
Riley N
Queensland, Australia

Dear Sister,

My name is Arlen. I'm a 32-year-old Brazilian, and I would like to share a little bit of my life history with you.

I graduated with a bachelor's degree in human resources management and a master's degree in business pedagogic. During the last six years, I have been working at social institutions that provide vocational training for young people and adults in the outskirts of the city São Paulo in Brazil. I'm also a worship leader at my local church and am part of a gospel band called "Rendição" (meaning "Surrender") with six other girls. It is a band that was initiated as part of a young singles ministry.

When I was invited to write to you about my life, I felt joyful and honored. I want to begin by saying this: you are not alone.

I grew up in an extremely sensual culture where the physical body is worshipped and women have to be sexy like the Carnaval goddesses. In this culture, if you walk down the street and no man says, "Hey gorgeous," "Hey hottie," or anything similar to that, then you are not pretty or beautiful enough. You are "below the standards."

I had an encounter with Jesus when I was 15 years old. It was then I learned that the beauty of a woman is in her fearing God. It is from the inside out (Proverbs 31:30). Friends and family would question me about this. Why did I, young and beautiful, become a believer? But I was happy and very much in love with Jesus, determined to follow Him and live a life with Him.

As the years passed, I had a desire to meet someone to date and marry. After all, I believe that every girl, deep down inside her heart, has the dream of being "happy ever after." But, I decided to wait on God and live the verse that says, "*An unmarried woman or virgin is concerned about the Lord's affairs: Her aim is to be devoted to the Lord in both body and spirit. But a married woman is concerned about the affairs of this world -how she can please her husband*" (1 Corinthians 7:34 NIV).

So, I was living to be concerned about the things of the Lord, to please Him, and to have an intimate and sincere relationship with Him. I spent a lot of personal time alone with the Lord - not only to pray and read the Bible, but also to go to the movies, have dinner, go to the park, travel, etc. During that time, He became more real to me. He became part of my life not only during church, but full time, at all the times.

As our relationship became more intimate, He, the Lord, healed me from my traumas, wounds, hurts and emotional needs. He was healing my emotions and character and molding me according to His word.

The more pressure that was put on me to get involved with a man, the more I would get involved with Jesus. I was willing to wait for a relationship that glorified the Lord at the right time. I graduated from college, went to Africa and to the Northeast of Brazil on mission trips, took classes, served in church, and served people. I worked hard, while always looking at Him.

I will soon be 33, and I'm not yet married. I surely do not feel sad, desperate, ugly, or anything similar to this, for I have found contentment in the Lord before finding it in a man, relationship, or any other earthly thing. I am still working, studying, praising Jesus, and carrying this message of peace, wait, and trust in the Lord with my life and testimony.

My sister, nothing in the whole world will satisfy you as the Lord does. All sources are found in Him. Wherever you are, I want to invite you to open that big smile not only in your face, but also in your heart. Have the conviction that:

- The fact that you are single is a great opportunity for you to build a deep and strong relationship with the Father.

- Building a relationship with a man before finding satisfaction in God will cause you to be in a relationship with someone for the wrong reasons, and this will certainly hurt you.

- You are beautiful and loved by God. Nothing can change this truth.

With the love of God,
Arlen Gomes
São Paulo, Brazil

Dear Sister,

I started dating when I turned 18. From then until my late 20s, I was rarely without a boyfriend. Most of my relationships lasted more than two years and, on occasion, I'd have a rebound guy between breakups. #ThankYouJesusForGrace

When God called me to build the kingdom and invest in my spiritual life by applying for an internship at church, I had already been single for nearly two years. My journey as a 30-year-old single intern started, and I committed to remaining single for the two-year internship.

My first Valentine's Day as a committed single woman was daunting. For the first time in years, I did not receive any flowers, chocolates, gifts, or trinkets - not even a special message. I'd never made a fuss about "the love day" in the past, but I felt a little sad for some reason. I guess the realization that I was 30 and single dawned on me and somehow unsettled my heart.

The scripture in Matthew 6:33, *"Seek the kingdom of God above all else, and live righteously, and he will give you everything you need,"* made me more determined to persist in my commitment.

Family gatherings didn't make it easier. The twenty questions from everyone drove me insane. Why are you single? When are you getting married? What are you waiting for? You are too picky!

The answer that I am content and committed to waiting on God's timing was incomprehensible to them. What God speaks in the heart of men, no one can understand (1 Corinthians 2:11).

When my sister got married, it didn't aid my stance. She is nine years younger than me. Most my friends are married, and I've been a bridesmaid more times than I could've imagined. This sometimes made me feel despondent and lonely.

Society has always seemed to dictate that being married equates to a successful life. In my opinion, a successful life is when you reach your goals and dreams based on God's timing, not on a timeline that society has set.

During the internship, I grew spiritually and God healed my heart of all past hurts. It was like He literally performed heart surgery. In a loving environment, I was able to address insecurities that had been hidden in my previous relationship statuses. I discovered a new passion for my dreams and started to actively pursue them. I became more independent and confident as I got to know who I am in Christ. Thanks to meditating on Psalm 139, I fell in love with myself, my body, and every quirky part of me because I was made in His image. Being single enabled me to fully tap into my potential and the purpose God has planned for my life. I've been able to pursue dreams that I had put on the backburner.

Over the last five years, I've been blessed to experience God's intimate love for me. He is my Father, my Lord, and my one true hope. He spoils me, He comforts me, He gives me joy,

He respects me, He guides me, and He challenges me to be the woman He has called me to be.

If I had been in a relationship during that time, I believe I would not have been able to fall in love with Christ in this personal and intimate way. It is my daily prayer that God does not awaken love in my heart until it so desires. I want to be fully ready and mature when entering into marriage.

When you know your worth and have Jesus in your life, you become content and have a peace that surpasses all understanding.

Lots of love,
Helouise
Cape Town, South Africa

Sisters,

What an honor it is to have the opportunity to share my experiences of being "30, Single, and I Don't Care." I reassure you that if you've found yourself with any association to this book title, whether "24, Single, and Mad", "37, Single, and Trying to Cope", or "56, Single, and in Disbelief", God is aware and sincerely loves you exactly where you are. Nothing in your situation is by mistake or surprise to Him. He is with you in this very moment and knew you would be reading this book to bring righteous perspective to your life.

Being single, we have the opportunity to devote unlimited attention to our purpose, no matter our age. We have no interruptions to attend to a spouse. If you have a child or children, you have the opportunity to gain righteous perspective in your position as a parent while also being an example of being whole in Christ alone. Having a healthy single experience is paramount to developing and managing effective use of your time on this earth. We can fully discover who we are as individuals, the details of our purpose, and what God has intended for His use through us.

There are many people who are married and have no idea of who they are as individuals or of their respective purpose. As singles, we have the opportunity to discover that without haphazard interruptions and distractions that happen within marriage. We can listen to God and truly learn His voice instead of continuing to submit to the enemy's. We are actually purposed and purposeful in our current position. We should not care about the world's goals and the associated timetables.

Many people like to discount being single as a "season." Although I understand where many are coming from with using this descriptor, it becomes an assumption that being single is supposed to end as fast as summer or winter. From this mindset, people can easily become disgruntled with being single if it exceeds their expectations of a season, whether it's been three months, two years, or even ten years. When the time of being single extends the time you've considered to be a season, the flesh becomes frustrated and flares up. This is why it is important to have the righteous perspective of keeping our eyes to Christ throughout our life and soaking up every detail of our purpose. The fulfillment of our purpose in God, what He's asked us to do in our lives, should always be more satisfying to us than our relationship status. This is what gives us the notion of not caring! Doing what God says should always be more satisfying than fulfilling the flesh. If it's not, you love people and your flesh more than God - and that's idolatry. That's another book for another day.

As long as we are being obedient to God, there is NO SUCH THING as time wasted or missing. We will trust His plan. God is the author of time. He knows how long you've been single. An earthly season (winter, spring, summer, fall) does not define your singleness, nor does it limit God!

I know personally how it feels to have heard all of this what seems like a million times. Although it is exact truth, we tend to allow our flesh to take control and grow weary with not having what we think we should. Everyone also likes to add their own opinions to your situation. "Be content. You have so much time on your hands to do what you want to do." Especially when you don't have children, the first thing someone says is often something like, "Oh! You don't have kids? You must have so much time on your hands. You need to be happy you're not married and don't have kids."

Also, if you're single, there are often very real and automatic assumptions that you're a workaholic, that something is wrong with you, or that you're bored out of your mind, twiddling your thumbs waiting to change your status from single to married. Yes, I know how it feels to be defined in each one of these categories. The takeaway and answer to all of this is that, "I am who God says I am, and God has a plan way bigger than my basic thoughts and plans for my life." Declare this over yourself daily and use it against any additives that people try to speak over your life.

I once had a plan that I would complete graduate school, get engaged, and be married by 24 years old. I'm now 29, turning 30 in two months, and the plan that I'm living now, "29, Single, and Purposed," is lightyears better than the basic life I once desired for myself. I would've been working in my career during the day and worshipping who I thought would be my husband by night. My relationship was my god. Well, when God calls you to truly belong to Him and you answer the call with a "Yes!", He will quickly show you that He is a jealous

God and will shut down any plans that are not the best for your life. That's exactly what He did to me! The same year I was to wed (in my mind), the Lord stripped me of my favorite form of idolatry, my relationship, that had been lord over my life for years!

The pain sucked. The tears cried were tremendous, and I often felt like I was dying. The truth of the matter was that I was dying! I was dying to myself and being shaped in God's image. As I prayed for Him to return me back to my "love," He was working on my heart to return me back to His love. Looking back, it was the most beautiful exchange. This intimate exchange took a solid three to four years. It is true that, *"The Lord is near to the broken-hearted and saves those who are crushed in spirit"* (Psalm 34:18 NIV). He reconciled me and restored me.

During this restoration time, I began to learn who God created me to be instead of what man desired for me. This happened spiritually and physically. I began to learn little things about myself, like what foods make my skin glow, the exact amount of sleep that I need to be functional, which spiritual disciplines make me feel most connected to God, what time alone with Him is like, and what conditions I need within my surroundings in order to think and hear clearly. These are random but good examples of characteristics that you can find out about yourself when you have time alone as a single.

In addition, you learn about what you're truly passionate about. Is there a certain profession that God has been calling you to, but you've rejected it because it is lower or uncertain pay? Are you being disobedient in your purpose because of what people might say? Do you submit to Christ, or do you still suffer from bondage to people? Are you content in your current position while being ready to hear and receive instructions to move at any given moment? Have you gained a sensitivity in hearing from God? These are all awesome qualities that you learn about and develop in while being single.

Being "Almost 30, Single, and Not Caring," I've had the opportunity to learn about my passions for serving people, travel, cooking, fashion, and design. I am constantly developing and refining these skills with a plethora of opportunities God has freely given me. Had I lived the plan that I thought I needed, I would have never learned who I was in Him, the many purposes He has for my life, and the ways He intends for those to glorify His kingdom.

One of the most AMAZING gifts I received in the past year was the vision for my company, Queenship Restored, LLC. It started out with a vision of writing a book and incorporating one of my passions, art, on the cover. Then another vision was given to incorporate another passion, fashion, to visually express the meanings of the art and books as wearable goods. Now, the point of explaining this quick story is not at all to highlight me but to highlight God's timing and the importance of keeping my eyes on Him. Had I been distracted with anything else in my life, particularly a relationship or marriage, I know I would've missed the visions and plans that God has ordained for me to impact way more people for His kingdom than I could have ever imagined.

The beautiful thing is that He used passions I discovered in my singleness to glorify Him in an unimaginable way. Don't miss this. I've had the opportunity for God to show Himself in me. Meaning, by giving Him all of me, He has been able to reveal to me the "beauty and wonder" (Psalm 139:14) that He has made uniquely within me for His purpose in my life. A spouse was not required for this revealing, only God. If you're single and feeling like you are not purposed until you're married, the devil is lying to you. You have uninterrupted time and opportunity to clearly hear from God with no human distractions. As Paul said, you have the divine opportunity to focus solely on the desires of God without being confounded with a spouse and their concerns (1 Corinthians 7:32-35).

Thus, as Jules has written, you should not care what the world says your relationship status should be at this point. There are enough women and men under and over 30 that are married and have no idea of who they are, what God has purposed them to do, and what it means to be whole in Christ alone. Being in that position and having a spouse, because the world says we need one out of God's timing, is tormenting to the person and their spouse. Don't be that person.

190

So, I pray that you come to the knowledge of the truth that your life is valuable and purposeful. Your status of being single or married never will be a defining moment in your life. Your relationship goals not being achieved by your desired age does not define you. You are only defined by God through the fulfillment of your purpose here on earth. So, if you can relate to any of this that has been written, be +/- 30, single, and don't care.

I love you and am believing God for the restoration of your mind and heart. If He did it for me, He can do it for you.

Sincerely,
April D. Wesley
Atlanta, Georgia, US